Unlearned Lessons

Unlearned Lessons

Current and Past Reforms for School Improvement

Barbara Z. Presseisen

 The Falmer Press

(A member of the Taylor & Francis Group)
Philadelphia and London

UK   The Falmer Press, Falmer House, Barcombe, Lewes, East Sussex, BN8 5DL

USA   The Falmer Press, Taylor & Francis Inc., 242 Cherry Street, Philadelphia, PA 19106-1906

Copyright © Research for Better Schools, Inc. 1985

First published 1985

Library of Congress Cataloging in Publication Data

Presseisen, Barbara Z.
  Unlearned Lessons.

  Bibliography: p.
  Includes index.
  1. Education—United States—Aims and Objectives.
2. Public Schools—United States.   I. Title.
LA217.P74   1985   370′.973   85-20659
ISBN 1-85000-079-4
ISBN 1-85000-080-9 (pbk.)

Jacket design by Caroline Archer

Jacket illustration: *School's Out,* a lithograph by Howard Baer, reproduced here by kind permission of the artist and Associated American Artists, New York.

Typeset in 11/13 Bembo by
Imago Publishing Ltd, Thame, Oxon.

Printed in Great Britain by Taylor & Francis (Printers) Ltd, Basingstoke

Contents

TO ERNST

who shares my love of learning

An ancient Sumerian riddle

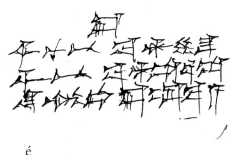

é
igi-nu-bad ba-an-tu
igi —bad ba-an-ta-è
ki-húr-bi é-dub-ha-a

A house —
One whose eyes are not open, entered it,
One whose eyes are open, went out of it.
Its solution — A school.

C.J. Gadd and S.N. Kramer, *Ur Excavation Texts* (1966), Plate CCLXIV no. 341

Acknowledgments

There are many persons who have helped make this volume possible and to whom I am indebted for their assistance and encouragement.

Research for Better Schools (RBS) recognized the importance of studying reform periods in education and enabled me to conduct the research that is the foundation of the study. John Hopkins, John Connolly and Louis Maquire were supportive of my efforts. Members of the Urban Development staff at RBS — Tom Corcoran, Rima Miller, Joe D'Amico, Michele Woods and Judy Dawson — interacted with me often on the research issues and on implications of reform recommendations for actual school practice. I am particularly grateful to Marian Chapman, Director of the Resource Center at RBS, who reviewed the initial manuscript and made many constructive recommendations. Peter Donahoe of the Resource Center staff was invaluable in helping me locate extensive resources and I am continously appreciative of his cheerful assistance. Last among staff at RBS, but hardly least, I must commend Maria Omar-Waters who typed the manuscript several times over. Not quite as put upon as Tolstoy's wife (who wrote out *War and Peace* thirteen times in longhand!), Maria had the benefit of modern word processing, but her skill and especially her wonderful disposition are most appreciated. Doris L. Harris readily helped in the typing task as well.

The National Institute of Education (NIE) supported RBS in the completion of this research and indicated their long-term interest in the improvement of education. To NIE Project Officer Cheryl P. Garnette, I would like to express my gratefulness. Mr. Thomas Seagears of the Department of Education was helpful in obtaining copyright authorization.

The role of editor should never be underestimated. I am particularly appreciative of the fine skills of Üllik Rouk who was my major editor and intellectual critic. Üllik's knowledge of educational issues and her particular ability to craft clarity and conciseness helped construct a book from the initial manuscript.

Ted Sizer read the study and was very helpful in making suggestions about ways to approach the final design. Samuel Noah Kramer kindly located and translated the Sumerian riddle used in the dedication. Joseph T. Freeman, M.D. shared his lovely lithograph, *School's Out*, by Howard Baer for the cover and Associated American Artists arranged the reproduction rights.

I am grateful to the Thinking Skills Committee of the Association for Supervision and Curriculum Development (ASCD) for helping me see the new interest in thinking and problem solving as a major issue in the current reform period. Ron Brandt, Art Costa, and John Barell have been particularly helpful. Staff persons working on thinking skills at the school districts of Philadelphia and Baltimore — Kathy Connor, Earline Sloan, Robin Hobbs and Mary Ann Brearton — have been most informative in seeing this issue from the practitioner's perspective. Jay McTighe of the Maryland State Department of Education and John Meehan of the Pennsylvania Department of Education have generously offered their views from the state's interest.

Finally, I must thank my husband, Ernst Presseisen, and our sons, Joshua and Benjamin, for their encouragement of my research and for their affirmation of what an inquiring life can be. If teaching is a great part of parenting, which I suggest in the book, we all share the educative experience and know how important it is to a productive existence.

Barbara Z. Presseisen
Philadelphia, Pennsylvania
March, 1985

Abbreviations

The following is a list of abbreviations used in the text.

ACT	American College Test
AFDC	Aid to Families with Dependent Children
AFT	American Federation of Teachers
ASCD	Association for Supervision and Curriculum Development
BSCS	Biological Sciences Curriculum Study
ESEA	Elementary and Secondary Education Act
ERIC	Educational Resources Information Center
G.I. BILL	Government Issue, legislation regarding military veterans
IQ	Intelligence Quotient
MACOS	Man a Course of Study
NAEP	National Assessment of Education Progress
NAIS	National Association of Independent Schools
NASSP	National Association of Secondary School Principals
NEA	National Education Association
NIE	National Institute of Education
PSSC	Physical Science Study Committee
RBS	Research for Better Schools, Inc.
SAT	Scholastic Aptitude Test
SCIS	Science Curriculum Improvement Study
SMSG	School Mathematics Study Group
YMCA	Young Men's Christian Association

List of Figures

Prologue

The American experiment in democracy depends on the potential of free and independent human beings. That potential can be expressed in various ways: through creativity, social interactions, aspirations, and dreams of a better future. Education — the development of mental and moral qualities, especially through schooling — is an essential ingredient in realizing the potential of all America's citizens. This has been a central theme throughout the history of the Republic. Education today is regarded as both a measure of success for the individual citizen and an investment in human resources for the society at large.

How does American education fare at the end of the twentieth century? Are we accomplished or mediocre? Can we move forward assured of our national goals or are we confused and ill-directed? Do we delude ourselves with myths or are we brave enough to renew national purposes for the benefit of all?

The most important thing, it would seem, is that we dare to examine, to question, to raise the possibility of educational reform and ultimate change. From such a self-examination, as the founders of the Republic so aptly decreed, we can 'submit our facts to a candid world'.

Introduction

Plus que change, c'est la même chose.

The more things change, the more they are the same.

Alphonse Karr, *The Home Book of Quotations* (1967)

American educators do some soul searching about the state of the nation's schools about every twenty or twenty-five years. Commission reports and prestigious studies are produced; recommendations and guiding principles are promulgated. It is the beginning of another era of educational reform.

Today we are engaged in just this kind of experience. The work initiated in 1983 by the National Commission on Excellence in Education, established by US Secretary of Education Terrel H. Bell, has been joined by dozens of studies and reports conducted by formidable panels and renowned scholars. What messages do these august bodies bring to teachers, administrators, and supervisors in American schools? What direction do these critiques provide to parents and community leaders?

Assessing a period of educational reform is a historic problem. Today's reform recommendations are another link in a chain of improvement efforts that began nearly a century ago. The current wave of reform proposals is also the product of various organizations and institutions, each with its own perspective and interpretation of the needs of American society at this moment in history.

Periods of reform wax and wane according to current events. At the beginning of 1985, Secretary Bell resigned and William J. Bennett was named his successor. What will be the fate of educational reform? Will the reports of the eighties merely gather dust on library shelves or be relegated to obscurity behind an ERIC document number? It all depends on how seriously this period of educational evaluation is taken by the nation and its educators. To ignore the current reports, to fail to reflect on their recommendations and to deliberate their meanings will be to lose an opportunity that may not return in this century. Lessons about how the nation perceives its educational mission and what the citizenry thinks ought to be the outcomes of schooling will go unlearned. Just as we have failed to build an understanding of reform periods since the work of the Committee of Ten at the end of the nineteenth century, unlearned lessons about the reforms of eighties will fade into our country's future. Unexamined will be the rich literature that has emerged in response to reform recommendations. Unexplored will be the reasons why such suggestions could or could not resolve the issues deliberated.

George Santayana warned that those who ignore history are doomed to repeat its mistakes. To a large extent, this is the case with reform literature in American education. Tanner (1982) suggests that reform eras arise as crises because problems reoccur but never get resolved. Comparing the current reports to their predecessors as well as to each other is, in part, an effort to avoid that historical pitfall. That is the major focus of this book. Eight recent critiques of American education are reviewed in order to sample their arguments in assessing schooling. There is also an examination of historical underpinnings of the current reports and past experiences at improving education (see Figure 1).

The historian takes a long-range view of phenomena. Patterns of consistency and change over time are the usual bases for analyzing particular events. Reform movements in American education are no exception. During each period of educational redefinition, similar issues emerged. But, at the same time, different periods exhibited particular problems and changing conditions which required solutions unique to the times. What are the patterns of consistency and change that underlie the reform reports of the eighties? How do conditions differ today from other reform eras and what constraints or possibilities do present circumstances offer for resolving educational problems? What, indeed, considering historic perspectives, are the educational problems that need to be addressed for America's future? These questions are central to analyzing the eight reform reports reviewed in this book.

Unlearned Lessons is divided into three sections. Part One examines the significance of the reports of the eighties and reviews previous reform periods of educational reform. Part Two focuses on eight major

Figure 1:   The Eight Reports Reviewed in This Study*

A Nation at Risk: The Imperative for Educational Reform.
National Commission on Excellence in Education, Washington, D.C.: Government Printing Office, 1983.

The Paideia Proposal: An Educational Manifesto.
Mortimer J. Adler on behalf of the members of the Paideia Group, New York: Macmillan Publishing Co., Inc., 1982.

High School: A Report on Secondary Education in America.
Ernest L. Boyer, New York: Harper & Row Publishers, 1983.

Academic Preparation for College: What Students Need to Know and Be Able to Do.
New York: The College Board, 1983.

Action for Excellence: A Comprehensive Plan to Improve Our Nation's Schools.
Washington, D.C.: Task Force on Education for Economic Growth, Education Commission of the States, 1983.

Making the Grade: Report of the Twentieth Century Fund Task Force on Federal Elementary and Secondary Education Policy.
New York: The Twentieth Century Fund, 1983.

Educating Americans for the 21st Century: A plan of action for improving mathematics, science and technology education for all American elementary and secondary students so that their achievement is the best in the world by 1995.
Washington, D.C.: National Science Board Commission on Precollegiate Education in Mathematics, Science and Technology, National Science Foundation, 1983.

Horace's Compromise: The Dilemma of the American High School.
Theodore R. Sizer, Boston: Houghton Mifflin Company, 1984.

*Information cited in these eight studies will refer to the report by title; other information attributed to the reports' authors or to the commissions will be cited accordingly.

studies of the current period. Citations illustrate the language of the writers and capture the basic organization or approach of a study. General understandings of the current reform literature are used to analyze the reform movement of the eighties, and each report is assessed according to its philosophic and historic view of schooling. A comparative analysis of current reform reports documents discrete problems. Part Three concentrates on the problems that emerge from analyzing the reports. Lessons for the future of American education are drawn on the basis of historic conditions and with respect to findings in current educational research and practice. Finally, the impact of the reform reports is assessed and prospects for long-term change and renewal in American education are examined.

Part I
Historic Underpinnings

1 The Significance of Educational Reform

> Whether or not, as Emerson once forecast, the time will come when education supersedes politics as the fundamental mode of human affairs, education has already preceded and set the stage for politics at several critical turning points in the nation's history.
>
> Lawrence A. Cremin, *Traditions of American Education* (1977)

There is a tendency for every age to think itself unique. In one sense, at least, this is true. Each age has its own conditions, people, and relationships that make it different from every other age. It is the same with educational reform periods. The reforms of the eighties create an atmosphere of expectation. Something new and different is being elicited from American education under circumstances that the country has never faced before.

Reform and Public Conscience

The educational studies that have appeared over the past two years are notable for their bulk and extensiveness, if not for their wisdom. The eight reform reports reviewed here are formidable output from prestigious commissions, leaders, and organizations in American education. They are significant not only because they thrust education into the national spotlight, but also because they display the enormous energy and commitment that various segments of society have invested in improving elementary and secondary schooling. Because they address society-at-large, they are not in-house documents meant solely for a professional readership, they have forced education into the American mainstream. That is both good and bad news for educational improvement.

Never before has American education triggered such extensive public discussion. Even though the reports were usually issued as reprimands, the public consensus was 'yes, we've slipped; so let's change our ways' (Yudof, 1984). Authors of the various studies have been deluged with speaking requests. In 1983 and 1984, conventions, television talk shows, and personal appearances made school reform a 'media event' (Toch, 1984). The positive side of this is that for the first time in the country's history the full force of the nation's vast communications network has been brought to bear on the nation's schools. Like the selling of the presidency, the selling of public education has finally become a reality. The danger, unfortunately, is that the opportunity for reform could be lost just as quickly as the next hot public issue supercedes educational change.

The reform reports have sensitized 'individuals and groups to changing conditions and forces and to the urgency for change in the institutions and agencies concerned with the education of youth' (Passow, 1976, p. 54). But such sensitivity carries with it a responsibility to find appropriate pathways to change. Have the auspicious commissions succeeded at this task? Have they created the means for others to do so? Consider reactions to the reports.

Critics of Reform

Some writers deplore the attention given the reform literature because of the pressure it generates for immediate improvement (Albrecht, 1984). Sarason (1983), commenting on the current indictment of schools, points out that generations of Americans have looked to schooling as a vehicle for secular salvation, and when that failed they quickly made schools scapegoats for society's ills. Other writers suggest that naming prestigious commissions prior to an election year was a political move, not an educational one, and that such appointments are inappropriate to the real task at hand (Peterson, 1983). The underlying argument of many of these criticisms is that school improvement is not amenable to 'quick-fix' solutions. Unless ideas and actions are carefully thought out and researched, they are liable to be ill-conceived. Albrecht (1984) contends that the publicity surrounding *A Nation at Risk* obscures the more thoughtful and imaginative reports written by Boyer and Sizer. Leonard's (1984) inclination is that most of the commissions' work is old hat and rather shallow. Peterson (1983) concurs, noting that prestigious commissions could hardly do otherwise because their very nature precludes them from taking the time or doing the indepth research required to produce meaningful studies.

Stedman and Smith's (1983) analysis of reform literature speaks to the problem of addressing the reports as reasoned documents. These researchers maintain that the four studies they reviewed (*A Nation at Risk, Action for Excellence, Academic Preparation for College* and *Making the Grade*) fall short mainly because 'they present a litany of charges without examining the veracity of their evidence and its sources' (p. 87). Their conclusion is the result of examining three arguments presented in the studies, and particularly brought out in *A Nation at Risk*. First, in looking at the evidence for the sad state of American education, Stedman and Smith found that, in some cases, the poor use of test data spawned unfounded conclusions. The researchers even go so far as to suggest that the authors of *A Nation at Risk* ignored the findings of their own commissioned studies in producing their report. Second, Stedman and Smith criticize the claim that the US education system is inferior to that of other countries on the grounds that such a comparison is inadequate and the data ill-sought. And third, they question the veracity of the reports' contention that a 'high-tech' revolution is sweeping the American economy. The change, they say, is really more complex than the reports describe and involves other conditions that also have to be taken into account in shaping plans for school improvement — conditions such as the future job market, implications for job training, and the technology needs of education itself.

Stedman and Smith's critique parallels Peterson's (1983) line of sound policy analysis:

- presenting statements of the problem to be analyzed;
- conducting methodological evaluation of existing research;
- providing reasoned consideration of options; and
- presenting supporting evidence and argumentation for well-specified proposals. (p. 3)

But such analysis is exactly what national commissions are not geared to do. Stedman and Smith indicate that the purpose of the reform reports is to bring education to the consciousness of the public; the reports are polemics, statements designed to dramatize problems and to elicit solutions. And that is exactly what many commentators say the reports have done so well (Howe, 1983; Honig, 1984). Perhaps here lies the greatest value of the current reports: they have stirred the national conscience. Now, however, it is up to educators to seize the moment for real reform. Despite their public relations features, the reports of the eighties œan impel professional dialogue. They can, and to some extent already have, sparked meaningful debate about education at a time when real change appears feasible — at a 'critical turning point' in the nation's history. As Passow (1984) sees it, 'Many of the recommendations simply cannot be implemented but can serve to stimulate thoughtful reflection, study, and planning' (p. 680). Using the reports in this way requires careful reading and an examination of their recommendations from a long-range perspective as well as from a more immediate point of view.

Reform and National Debate

The literature on reform, then, is viable as a basis for deliberate, educational debate. Tyler (1982) suggests that reform periods usually emerge during times of economic recession, when it becomes necessary to examine the funds allocated to various educational activities (p. 655). Ideally, such examinations should also sort out which educational strategies have the most potential for student achievement and then target limited resources to them. To do this, of course, requires careful reading of what went wrong with the system in the first place. Stedman and Smith (1983) draw an extensive list of deficiencies:

> Our schools, historically, have failed to educate well a majority of our youth, whether this is measured by college graduation, the capacity to write a cogent essay, mastery of advanced mathematical and scientific concepts, training in literature and foreign languages, or the acquisition of higher-order reasoning and problem solving skills. This in itself should be sufficient motivation for change. (p. 94)

Better communication among the various interest groups in American education may be an important by-product of reform deliberation. A deeper understanding of the history of American education, especially of reform periods, may be another, albeit unintended, outcome. But there must also be a third effect. This may be a greater understanding of the American nation itself, based on the ways it seeks to alter the education of its youth. Finkelstein (1984) puts it this way:

> For when Americans set about the work of constructing and reconstructing their public schools, they discover, define, and

reveal their collective commitments. Indeed, education reform proceeds in a political web of such exquisite complexity and sensitivity that generations of public school reformers, in order to generate political support, have had to discover harmonies of interest among a diverse and contentious people. (p. 275)

2   *Past Reform Periods*

Despite the existence of free, universal and compulsory schooling, most poor
children become poor adults. Schools are not great democratic engines for
identifying talent and matching it with opportunity. The children of the
affluent by and large take the best marks and the best jobs.

Michael B. Katz, *Class, Bureaucracy, and Schools* (1975)

Several months before the release of *A Nation at Risk,* James and Tyack
(1983) suggested that America could learn a lot from past efforts to
reform high schools. High schools have long been the focal point of
reform. Perhaps more than any other institution, they are the intimate
link between youthful dreams and real-world opportunities.

The Committee of Ten and Elitism

Nearly 100 years ago, in 1893, a committee of college presidents and
professors met under the auspices of the National Education Association (NEA) to impose a common college preparation on what they
saw as an unruly, rapidly expanding secondary education system. The
group, which became known as the Committee of Ten, created a series
of sub-committees in various curricular programs (classical, Latin/
scientific, modern languages, and English) whose task was to specify
desirable content, in order of difficulty, within each program. After,
several conferences and a great deal of debate, four uniform programs
were established[1] to ensure the development of high intellectual ability
among college-bound youth. The Committee planned that these
programs:

would all be taught consecutively and thoroughly, and would
all be carried on in the same spirit; they would all be used for

training the powers of observation, memory, expression, and reasoning; and they would all be good to that end, although differing among themselves in quality and substance. (Hahn and Bidna, 1965, pp. 165–6)

The Chairman of the Committee of Ten was Charles William Eliot, President of Harvard University. Although Eliot and his colleagues were primarily concerned with intellectually gifted students whose parents could afford to send them to Ivy League institutions, they were not totally devoid of a democratic conscience. The Committee still considered the main function of high school the preparation of students for the duties of life (Hahn and Bidna, 1965). By creating a standard curriculum for college admission, they hoped to draw out those elite young men earmarked for 'challenging careers emerging in a complex and interdependent society' (James and Tyack, 1983, p. 402). The plan was reinforced a short time later when the Carnegie Foundation defined educational units and colleges and universities began to grant credit for secondary school courses deemed acceptable for admission to higher education. 'The Carnegie Unit' has been the curricular currency of college admission ever since.

The Cardinal Principles and Progressivism

Twenty-five years after the Committee of Ten fixed college admission standards, the NEA sponsored another educational panel, the Commission on the Reorganization of Secondary Education. This group, chaired by Clarence D. Kingsley, State Supervisor of High Schools in Massachusetts, was distinctly different from President Eliot's Committee. Members of the Commission included 'three education professors, a university president who had recently been an education professor, the US Commissioner of Education, two state high school supervisors, a normal school principal, a representative from a private school, and a YMCA secretary' (James and Tyack, 1983, p. 403). The Commission's report, titled *The Cardinal Principles of Secondary Education*, was issued in 1918. It heralded a new approach to secondary schooling.

The Cardinal Principles focused on the dynamic needs of democratic society. As 'society is always in process of development', said the Commission, the high school program must reorganize at irregular intervals. After examining the educational needs of citizens in the midst of fighting a Great War, the Commission established seven goals for secondary schooling: health, command of fundamental processes, worthy home-membership, vocation, civic education, worthy use of leisure and ethical character (Hahn and Bidna, 1965). The Commission's report provided an early example of social engineering; that is, using education to ameliorate social ills. The emphasis, even in the three Rs, was on practical matters.

> Much of the energy of the elementary school is properly devoted to teaching certain fundamental processes, such as reading, writing, arithmetic computations, and the elements of oral and written expression. The facility that a child of 12 or 14 may acquire in the use of these tools is not sufficient for the needs of modern life. This is particularly true of the mother tongue. Proficiency in many of these processes may be increased more effectively by their application to new material than by the formal reviews commonly employed in grades seven and eight. Throughout the secondary school, instruction and practice must go hand in hand, but as indicated in the report of the Committee on English, only so much theory should be taught at any one time as will show results in practice. (*Ibid*, p. 171).

The Cardinal Principles was a reaction against the prescribed classical curriculum of the Eliot Committee. Its writers fought educational elitism, sought to discredit older notions of discipline and training 'faculties of the mind', and rallied around the new field of educational science. They supported their arguments with writings, both old and new: Herbert Spencer's *What Knowledge Is of Most Worth?* had appeared in England in the mid-1850s, causing educators to direct curricula to the needs of an industrialized society; John Dewey's works began appearing at the beginning of the twentieth century and promoted progressive education as an antidote to more formal and traditional approaches; Franklin Bobbitt's *The Curriculum* was published in 1918. The first book in its field, it introduced the concept of a life-activity curriculum based on objectives derived from human experience. It is not to say here whether or not these works were employed accurately. Nonetheless, it is clear that *The Cardinal Principles* reflected the needs of a new kind of population that was literally invading public schools. The number of students attending public secondary institutions doubled every decade from 1880 to 1930 (Douglass, 1964). Kingsley's Commission saw differentiation of course preparation and training for social adjustment as the keys to progress

for this burgeoning population. The bureaucratized school, adminis-
tered by a new breed of educational expert, was to become the
mechanism for realizing a progressive national educational dream.

The 1920s were marked by numerous and varied activities ascribed
to 'progressive education'. Some centered on the curricular revisions
contained in *The Cardinal Principles*. William Heard Kilpatrick, a
popular professor at Teachers College, Columbia University, advocated 'the project method' as the best educational approach for teaching
the young, 'rather than through what he derisively called "subject
matter fixed-in-advance"' (Ravitch, 1983, p. 50). Vocational education
became a legitimate focus for older students. Colleges of education
included topics like 'the child-centered schools' and 'education for
community needs' in their courses. But progressivism was not without
its critics. Ravitch (1983) reports that the era was faulted for a decrease
in the number of students enrolled in college preparatory courses and
for showing little evidence of actual social reform in the public schools.
There was, moreover, resistance from parents and teachers to many of
the educational practices employed in the progressive movement.
Change did not come easily to the nation's schools.

Reform Between the Wars

The next wave of educational reform occurred after the Great Depres-
sion and was as much the result of the nation's social and economic
condition as it was a reaction to progressivism. 'Hard times forced
educators to reexamine and reinterpret the historic function of public
schools' (James and Tyack, 1983, p. 404). The problems of youth,
unemployment, apathy and unrest, emerged as national concerns
during this period. The general opinion was that education was
necessary in order for the country to survive, but beyond that,
individual philosophies diverged. Progressives like Harl Douglass saw
innovative New Deal youth work programs the salvation of young
people with mediocre or inferior academic ability. His study, *Secondary
Education for Youth in Modern America*, was submitted to the American
Youth Commission of the American Council on Education in 1937.
Similar arguments for adjusting schooling to the real-life needs of
greater numbers of students came from NEA's Educational Policies
Commission and the National Association of Secondary School Principals (NASSP). Ravitch (1983) summarizes a study by B.L. Dodds
released by the NASSP in 1939:

Not many adults need specialized knowledge in mathematics and science, and only those who can profit by it should get it. Nor do they need a high level of reading comprehension, only enough to use as an 'essential tool' for newspaper and magazine fare ... the trouble with the academic curriculum was that it had fostered and definitely encouraged unrealistic ambitions and made too many 'unselected' youth aspire to enter managerial and professional jobs for which they were not fitted (p. 61).

Strangely, it was John Dewey himself who condemned the extreme application of progressivism as a misinterpretation of his writings. In 1938, Dewey published *Experience and Education* and countered many of the progressives' ideas about educational freedom. 'The only freedom that is of enduring importance is freedom of intelligence'. (Dewey, quoted in Ravitch, 1983, p. 59) not the activity which is based on whim and impulse, he cautioned. In the same publication, Dewey endorsed the notion of knowledge from the past guiding learning about the present and the future. Similarly, historian Charles Beard's study, *The Unique Function of Education in American Democracy*, which had appeared the year before, declared the major goal of schooling was the transmission of knowledge. These arguments further fired the controversy between progressives and traditionalists.

In 1938, the famous *Eight Year Study* was begun. Sponsored by the Commission of the Progressive Education Association on School and College Relations in collaboration with the Carnegie Corporation and the General Education Board, the study was conceived as an empirical research design. One of its major objectives was to compare the college success of graduates of thirty so-called 'progressive' schools to the success of graduates of more traditional educational programs. Proponents of progressive education concluded that 'on the whole, the students from the thirty schools were superior to the control group' (Hahn and Bidna, 1965, p. 197). Defending progressivism some twenty-five years later, Douglass (1964) retorted that the study 'established conclusively that no particular plan of college preparation, so far as subjects in high school are concerned, is superior to any other plan' (p. 111). Opposition to progressivism, he explained, occurred for the following reasons:

Opposition of the Intellectuals. The conclusions of this study [This Eight-Year Study] did not materially discourage the critics of reform of the curriculum, particularly those who might be classified as intellectuals, would-be intellectuals, or pseudo-intellectuals. They made many criticisms of the modern changes in the high school curriculum, and among the more commonly voiced were the following: [Excerpted]

1   Students in secondary schools in other countries, for example, Russia, Switzerland, France, England and Germany, are further along in the sciences and mathematics and foreign languages than students at a comparable stage in secondary schools in the United States.
2   Secondary schools are largely concerned with 'life adjustment' courses, which have little to do with developing the intellect or scientific or cultural knowledge.
3   Many high schools offer 'snap' courses.
4   The requirements for graduation do not ensure an adequate introduction to culture or a well-rounded education.
5   Inadequate provision is made in the curriculum for bright children.
6   The schools do not provide appropriate curriculum materials for the less able students.
7   The curriculum of most schools contributes to physical as well as intellectual flabbiness. (pp. 112–113)

Although he admitted that some criticism was probably justified, Douglass remained a staunch advocate of 'modern', progressive education. The issues that separated him from 'the intellectuals' persisted into the next decade. Americans, meanwhile, largely remained educationally divided until after the Second World War.

Changes Following World War II

In the late 1940s and early 1950s, America experienced educational expansion that took place at all levels of the American education system. Soldiers were returning to college on the G.I. BILL; population increases swelled elementary classrooms; the country was making unprecedented economic and industrial progress. One characteristic of this period was its strong support for Charles Prosser's 'life adjustment' education, an outgrowth of the *The Cardinal Principles* and progressive philosophy. Prosser's approach was credited by a 1949 US Office Education study as meeting the imperative needs of every youth, and presaged the appearance, in 1960, of *Goals for Americans*. This latter document states, 'Above all, schooling should fit the varying capacities of individuals' (American Assembly, 1960, p. 7). By the early 1950s, the modern education envisioned in 1918 had been fully developed. As Ravitch (1983) described it, this practical approach to schooling:

> was clearly identified with 'functional' teaching, which used everyday situations as the medium of instruction, with the purpose of changing students' attitudes and behavior to conform to social norms. The ideal was the well-adjusted student, who was prepared to live effectively as a worker, a home member, and a citizen. (p. 68)

But the prevailing philosophy soon changed. Criticism of this new round of progressivism was the favored sport of several well-known educational writers: Mortimer Adler, Edward Krug, I.L. Kandel, Arthur Bestor and Albert Lynd, to name a few. The titles of their works revealed their message: *The Cult of Uncertainty*, *And Madly Teach*, *Educational Wastelands*, and *Quackery in the Public Schools*. These critiques, combined with progressivism's own inability to respond to realities of a new era, may have sufficed to kill the movement, but in 1957 the launching of the Russian satellite, *Sputnik I*, dealt the final blow. The threat of Russian supremacy in outer space, as well as here on earth, raised new questions about the quality of American schooling and the ability of secondary schools to graduate students ready to compete in a world-wide arena.

The Response to Sputnik

Two Harvard scholars are generally considered instigators of educational reform in the 1960s. Harvard President James Bryant Conant, following in the tradition of Charles William Eliot, examined the American high school and issued a major report with recommendations for improvement. Conant's report, *The American High School Today*, was funded through a grant from the Carnegie Corporation of New York to the Educational Testing Service and published in 1959 under the auspices of the National Citizens Council for Better Schools. Meanwhile, independent of Conant's work, Jerome S. Bruner of Harvard's Psychology Department convened a meeting of scientists, educators and scholars at Woods Hole on Cape Cod, Massachusetts under the auspices of the Education Committee of the National Academy of Sciences. The purpose of this meeting was to discuss how science education might be improved in the nation's schools. Bruner's report, published in the spring of 1960, was named *The Process of Education*. These two writers and their studies did much to characterize educational reform in America over the next decade.

Conant's study called for making the comprehensive high school more efficient and strengthening its academic program. High schools, according to Conant, had a dual purpose: providing a sound general education for all students and sorting out young people for varied destinies. To this end, Conant made twenty-one specific recommendations. He wanted individualized programs as well as ability groupings; he advocated a required program for all students, but expected some students to learn marketable job skills as well; he expected schools to address the concerns of both very slow learners and academically talented ones. Conant's recommendations also covered organization of the school day, admission requirements for advanced academic courses, development of an academic honors list, and the introduction of developmental reading classes. Mindful of America's international role after World War II and the growing significance of science and technology, Conant called for better foreign language instruction in high schools and new science programs for all students. Another of his goals for schools was to tighten standards 'such that students with less than average ability would have difficulty passing the course' (p. 73). Finally, Conant expressed concern for the development of students' civic understanding. He urged a homeroom experience in all four years of high school, and a senior social studies course on the economic and political underpinnings of participatory democracy.

Conant's proposals were relatively conservative. He was convinced that 'American education can be made satisfactory without any radical changes in the basic pattern' (p. 96). For the most part, he addressed the recommendations to the citizenry, although formally the report was directed to school board members and school administrators. The closing paragraph captured much of how Conant thought things ought to be in education:

> I conclude by addressing this final word to citizens who are concerned with public education: avoid generalizations, recognize the necessity of diversity, get the facts about your local situation, elect a good school board, and support the efforts of the board to improve the schools. (p. 96)

At Bruner's Woods Hole meeting, thirty-four scientists and educators discussed the nature of knowledge, especially scientific knowledge, and how students learn the content and processes of various academic disciplines. Among the participants were ten psychologists, six mathematicians, five biologists, four physicists, three educators, two historians, two cinematographers, one classicist and one medical specialist. With the exception of Bärbel Inhelder of the Institute Rousseau in Geneva, Switzerland, all of the participants were American. Inhelder was a close associate of Swiss epistemologist Jean Piaget and, in large degree, Bruner's ultimate description of the educational process was based on Piaget's theory.

Bruner expounded on four themes in *The Process of Education:* the role of structure in knowledge development, the importance of a student's readiness for learning, the significance of intuition in productive and creative thinking, and the need for a desire to learn. Bruner (1960) was convinced, 'that intellectual activity anywhere is the same, whether at the frontier of knowledge or in a third-grade classroom' (p. 14) and asserted that 'virtually all of the participants agreed that not teaching devices but teachers were the principal agents of instruction' (p. 15). One area of controversy that did arise at Woods Hole was: Should the teacher be the main arbiter of how to present a subject or, should there be a massive effort to prepare films, television programs, 'instructional programs for teaching machines' (p. 16), tests, and other educational materials and then develop training programs to teach teachers how to use them? From the Woods Hole debate came the concept of 'teacher-proof' materials and from that, a decade of curriculum development and innovation.

Reform proposals by Conant and Bruner became springboards for a widespread professional activity that took place in the 1960s. University scholars developed new academic curricula that read like alphabet soup: SMSG, BSCS, SCIS, MACOS, and PSSC. Teachers flocked to summer workshops to upgrade their subject-area knowledge. Publishers scrambled to market extensive kits or packages of instructional materials. University professors — often of the liberal arts — became ultimate authorities on content, combining in their course guides both Conant's appeal for higher standards and Bruner's emphasis on the mature thinking of disciplinary specialists. But while all this was going on, the baby boom generation entered high school, major shifts occurred in American demographics, and anxieties both at home and abroad prompted new challenges to school reforms.

The twenty-five years since Conant and Bruner published their reports have witnessed a parade of issues and problems confronting American culture. As greater numbers of teenagers sought secondary schooling, educators were caught with having to cope with the diverse needs of a heterogeneous population. As James and Tyack (1983) point out, 'Blacks, Hispanics, women, the handicapped and other groups too long ignored in educational policy now demanded a say in shaping the high school' (p. 405). Other reforms were handed down by the courts, especially in matters of school finance, student rights, segregation rulings, treatment of the handicapped, and bilingualism. In 1973, many of these reforms found their way into the recommendations of a commission to reorganize secondary education established by the Charles F. Kettering Foundation (Brown, 1973). In 1974, the Panel on Youth of the President's Science Advisory Committee suggested the creation of specialized rather than comprehensive high schools, while still other recommendations called for smaller, more personalized secondary schools. Many of these changes incorporated Bruner's, concepts about learning and teaching. In the mid-1970s, however, Bruner's instructional philosophy was subjected to severe criticism by a member of Congress and came into conflict with the value perspective of some school boards and citizens. This kind of criticism of reform efforts, combined with declining SAT scores and scientific and technological developments worldwide, sparked new national concern about achievement and schooling. By the early 1980s, a new era of reform had begun. Most of its issues, however, hark back to 1893 — the first era of educational reform — and echo the hopes and fears of reformers ever since.

Note

1 See the four alternative programs designed by the Committee of Ten in Appendix A.

Part II

The Current Reports

3   Eight Reports Reviewed

For even those texts or archaeological documents which seem the clearest and
the most accommodating will speak only when they are properly questioned.

Marc Bloch, *The Historian's Craft* (1964)

In the space of just two years, from 1983 to 1985, dozens of studies on
American schooling appeared in professional and lay publications. *A
Nation at Risk: The Imperative for Educational Reform* became a nation-
wide best seller and other reviews of schooling, to greater or lesser
degrees, shared the limelight, Some of the reports emanated from
ongoing national commissions, some were from temporary task forces,
and still others from well-known scholars. The eight reports reviewed
in this chapter are a formidable sample of these three kinds of studies
and, more important, the critiques triggered the reform era of the
eighties.

It is not necessary to review every statement or report that makes
up the current wave of educational criticism. Nonetheless, reviewing
main arguments is valuable for discerning similarities and differences
among reports and, more importantly, developing a broader conception of American education in the final quarter of the twentieth
century. Placing this view within a larger historical context yields some
insight into the problems of, and perhaps even some remedies for,
American education.

The eight reports are not research documents in the usual sense of
the word. They are essentially position papers on 'what ought to be' in
American education according to the commission, foundation, or
organization that sponsored a specific examination.[1] Many of the
reports use data from a variety of sources, including site observations
and specially commissioned papers, but none claims a rigorous review
of the literature on school reform or strict adherence to a particular

methodology. The reports are reviewed here in an expository manner. The purpose of this procedure is to clarify the major arguments in each report, demonstrate the interests of the persons responsible for the study, and define the assumptions and viewpoints that underlie the arguments. This is the stuff of which reform literature is made.

A Nation at Risk: The Imperative for Educational Reform

The thirty-six-page report of the National Commission on Excellence in Education is terse and to-the-point. America is at risk 'because competitors throughout the world are overtaking our once unchallenged lead in commerce, industry, science and technological innovation' (Goldberg and Harvey, 1983, p. 15). Several reasons are given for the nation's inability to compete, and among them, an inadequate educational system is branded the most culpable. Education is the chief support that 'undergirds American prosperity, security, and civility' (*A Nation at Risk*, 1983, p. 5). The Commission's statement is assertive, at times almost militant; it demands performance and speaks about educational failure in an explicit, quantitative style borrowed from psychometric literature:

> Many 17-year olds do not possess the 'higher order' intellectual skills we should expect of them. Nearly 40 per cent cannot draw inferences from written material; only one-fifth can write a persuasive essay; and only one-third can solve a mathematical problem requiring several steps. (p. 9)

The report warns of both immediate and long-range dangers to America's economic standing in a technological world. It claims that high school graduates have fallen behind not only in meeting the nation's expectations but also in matching the achievements of preceding generations. The upward mobility that our pluralistic society has taken for granted is suddenly in doubt because public education is failing. To turn this perilous situation around, says the report, schools will have to be made 'excellent'.

> We define 'excellence' to mean several related things. At the level of the individual learner, it means performing on the boundary of individual ability in ways that test and push back personal limits, in school and in the workplace. Excellence

characterizes a school or college that sets high expectations and goals for all learners, then tries in every way possible to help students reach them. Excellence characterizes a society that has adopted these policies, for it will then be prepared through the education and skill of its people to respond to the challenges of a rapidly changing world. (p. 12)

A Nation at Risk is mindful of the difficulties that equity brings to bear on its educational goals but does not let this challenge interfere with the high expectations it has for *all* the nation's youth. At the heart of 'the learning society' is 'the commitment to a set of values and to a system of education that affords all members the opportunity to stretch their minds to full capacity, from early childhood through adulthood . . .' (p. 13). Life-long learning and high-quality schooling are the basis of 'the learning society'.

The main arguments in *A Nation at Risk* fall into five topic areas: content, standards and expectations, time, teaching, and leadership and fiscal support. Discussion of the first four areas focuses on inadequacies in the present educational system and recommendations for improvement. The fifth area, leadership and fiscal support, is left mainly to local initiatives. The report's recommendations are not directly related to the commissioned papers cited in the appendix.[2] Rather, it explains the philosophical premises upon which it bases its formal suggestions this way:

> Our recommendations are based on the beliefs that everyone can learn, that everyone is born with an urge to learn which can be nurtured, that a solid high school education is within the reach of virtually all, and that life-long learning will equip people with the skills required for new careers and for citizenship. (p. 24)

A Nation at Risk recommends course content in five 'New Basic' academic areas (English, mathematics, science, social studies, and computer science) as well as work in foreign languages, the arts, and vocational education. It advises elementary grades to prepare students for high school, and urges professional personnel to update their knowledge of subject matter. In general, it advocates stiffer high school graduation requirements, longer school days and years, more homework, a career ladder for teacher advancement, and more student testing and higher college admission standards, especially for prospective teachers. The report also calls for higher teacher salaries, but in return, wants more rigorous staff development and teacher evaluation. It places the burden of educational leadership on the entire school community, including local business. Authority for school improvement is clearly with local agencies; only limited assistance from the federal government is mentioned.

The Paideia Proposal: An Educational Manifesto

The Paideia Proposal actually appeared in print about six months before *A Nation at Risk*. It was published by a committee of twenty-two educators called the Paideia Group, headed by Mortimer J. Adler of the Institute for Philosophical Research in Chicago. The proposal is addressed to virtually every group of Americans concerned with the future of public schools: parents, teachers, school boards, college teachers, elected officials, employers, minority groups, labor and military leaders, and American citizens — including, of course, students themselves. A second publication, *Paideia Problems and Possibilities*, appeared in 1983.

Adler and his associates present a philosophy of schooling within a larger vision of bringing up children, as in the Greek *pais/paidos* (child/children). The program they propose is stated in manifesto style. It is clearly a polemic: it seeks to convince or persuade, with an aura of righteous determination. Several basic principles are woven throughout twelve chapters. They are:

- Every child is educable up to his or her capacity;
- The best education for the best is the best education for all;
- There are no unteachable children. There are only schools and teachers and parents who fail to teach them;
- Education is a lifelong process of which schooling is only a small but necessary part; and
- Schooling prepares the individual for further learning. (*The Paideia Proposal*, 1983)

Much of what Adler presents is reminiscent of the teachings of John Dewey, who is cited in the report frequently. Learning, according to the *The Paideia Proposal*, is an active engagement not a passive one. 'Doing' involves an interaction between the mind of the learner and the products of arts and sciences. *The Paideia Proposal* assumes that all children are born with the desire and the need to know, and that such natural curiosity can be either nourished or starved. The central task of schooling is to engage these natural abilities and interests, which, according to this document, differ among individuals in degree but not in kind.

> Only the student whose mind has been engaged in thinking for itself is an active participant in the learning process that is essential to basic schooling. (p. 32)

The heart of *The Paideia Proposal* is the same K-12 course of study for all students. This course contains three distinct modes of teaching and learning which correspond to three different ways in which the learner's mind can be improved:

- By the acquisition of organized knowledge;
- By the development of intellectual skills; and
- By the enlargement of understanding, insight, and aesthetic appreciation.

The content of schooling, the cognitive bases of learning, and the needs of the student are embedded in these goals. Specific content areas in each goal, instructional methods, and activities are delineated for each goal area. Figure 2 presents a synopsis of the ideal Paideia program.

Figure 2: The Same Course of Study for All: The Paideia Proposal (1983, p. 23.)

	COLUMN ONE	COLUMN TWO	COLUMN THREE
Goals	Acquisition of organized knowledge	Development of intellectual skills — skills of learning	Enlarged understanding of ideas and values
	by means of	by means of	by means of
Means	Didactic instruction lectures and responses textbooks and other aids	Coaching, exercises and supervised practice	Maieutic or Socratic questioning and active participation
	in three areas of subject-matter	in the operations of	in the
Areas Operations and Activities	Language, literature, and the fine arts mathematics and natural science history, geography, and social studies	Reading, writing, speaking, listening calculating, problem-solving, observing, measuring estimating, exercising critical judgment	Discussion of books (not textbooks) and other works of art and involvement in artistic activities, for example, music, drama visual arts

The three columns do not correspond to separate courses, nor is one kind of teaching and learning necessarily confined to any one class.

The Paideia Proposal envisions all three goals of schooling integrated at all grade levels. As students move from early grades to later ones, materials gradually become more complex. Similarly, a greater reliance on coaching and questioning techniques characterizes instruction of older, more able students.

The proposal is explicit about practices and procedures it considers dysfunctional to schooling. Tracking students, non-essential courses (including electives), job training, and joyless teaching are eliminated from the school's repertoire. A second language, physical education and health, limited manual activities, and some instruction in choosing and finding a career are included as auxiliary services of the school, but only to support the basic course of study. The proposal advises remediation whenever needed and strongly supports preschool education, especially for children from disadvantaged social and economic backgrounds.

Finally, *The Paideia Proposal* calls for expertly prepared teachers who are knowledgeable in the humanities and liberal arts. Its emphasis on teaching through coaching and questioning requires that teachers understand 'how the mind learns by the exercise of its own powers' (p. 61).. The principal's role in this is to be a headteacher who shows commitment to schooling and a sensitivity to the teaching-learning process. *The Paideia Proposal* also makes principals responsible for hiring or firing faculty, as well as for setting and enforcing standards of conduct in their buildings.

The report's authors see *The Paideia Proposal* as a radical plan for educational reform. They deny that the program is utopian and claim that it gives educators a framework for achieving improved student achievement. According to Adler, responsiveness is the greatest challenge facing educational reform. For the Paideia Group, how the challenge is met will determine the future of democratic society.

High School: A Report on Secondary Education in America

High School by Ernest L. Boyer is a report of the Carnegie Foundation for the Advancement of Teaching. It was completed with counsel from a National High School Panel representing professional educators, business executives, parent groups, and labor organizations. Boyer himself is a member of the Paideia Group.

The report is based on observations over a two-year period by twenty-five educators who visited fifteen pre-selected high schools across the country, a review of related educational literature, and numerous discussions with educators at all levels of the American school system. Boyer credits two research studies as being particularly helpful: John Goodlad's *A Study of Schooling* and James Coleman's *High School and Beyond*. Boyer himself does not consider his study a rigorous ethnographic document, but does contend that he and his team candidly assessed school conditions and used actual field materials in interpreting the status of public schooling. *High School* addresses its recommendations to the American citizenry-at-large and prevails upon the entire nation to reaffirm its 'historic commitment to public schools' (*High School*, 1983, p. xv).

High School is built around ten themes:

- To clarify the goals of education;
- To stress the centrality of language and link the curriculum to a changing national and global context;
- To recognize that all students must be prepared for a lifetime of both work and further education;
- To strengthen the profession of teaching in America. This means improvement of conditions in the classroom, better recruitment and preparation, better continuing education, and better teacher recognition and rewards;
- To improve instruction and give students more opportunities for service in anticipation of their growing civic and social responsibilities as they become adults;
- To take full advantage of the information revolution and link technology more effectively to teaching and learning in the schools;
- To smooth the transition from school to adult life through more flexible class scheduling and by making available to students new learning places both on and off the campus;
- To reduce bureaucracy in education and give school principals the support they need to lead;
- To recognize that excellence in education is possible only when connections are made with higher education and with the corporate world;
- Finally, the time has come for public schools to be aggressively supported by parents, school boards and government as well; and for the nation's historic commitment to public education to be vigorously reaffirmed by all. (p. 7)

The equity/quality dilemma in American schools arises early on. *High School* insists there is a national consensus that America's future depends upon public education but it does not place blame for mediocre performance, choosing instead to cast its argument in a more positive metaphor: 'There is a spreading awareness that every mind is a precious resource we cannot afford to waste' (p. 1). *High School* concedes that the push for educational excellence is linked to economic and political pressures, but refuses to separate these from the equity issues: 'Clearly, equity and excellence cannot be divided' (p. 6), declares the report. Expanding access to schooling for all students requires upgrading the quality of the entire program and making all students able to meet the academic challenge.

High School is organized into six sections. Part I, 'A Troubled Institution', is largely an anecdotal account of field observations and a discussion of standardized test scores over the past twenty years. Results from the SAT, the Iowa Test of Educational Development, and the National Assessment of Educational Progress (NAEP) are cited to show that, nationally, performance has fallen short of both public hopes and expectations. These findings are contrasted with Torsten Husén's comparison of American high school youth's achievement and that of students in thirteen other countries. *High School* notes:

> ... when the average scores of all students are compared, the United States youth performed poorly in most subjects. However, when only top students were rated, those in the United States compared more favorably with those in other countries. (p. 33)

Boyer suggests that America's educational performance is really mixed: historically this country has educated more immigrants at higher levels than any other nation in the world; but at the same time, it has been unable to achieve high academic results for many of its students. According to *High School*, low achievement scores, combined with family upheavals, economic disruptions, and political suspicions, make the time ripe for challenging the weak state of American education. The second section of the report, 'A Clear and Vital Mission', lays the groundwork for this confrontation.

High School traces the history of the American public high school from its origins in Boston in 1821 to the present day. It shows the tremendous expansion that was taking place in secondary schooling by the turn of the century and discusses curriculum developments and prestigious commissions that shaped how Americans learned. Curricu-

lum, in this report, is synonymous with courses or scholastic disciplines. Curricular changes over time reveal a dual trend in America's
high schools: hard subjects for the college-bound, other real-life
experiences for the less academically inclined. *High School* concludes
rather sympathetically that:

> Today's high school is called upon to provide the services and
> transmit the values we used to expect from the community and
> the home and the church. And if they fail anywhere along the
> line, they are condemned. (p. 57)

The report suggests that the obvious remedy for this sad state of
educational affairs is to reconceptualize the high school's mission. A
common vision must be formulated for everyone in the teaching-
learning process. That vision, says the report, rests on achieving four
essential goals:

- First, the high school should help all students develop the
  capacity to think critically and communicate effectively through
  a mastery of language;
- Second, the high school should help all students learn about
  themselves, the human heritage, and the interdependent world
  in which they live through a core curriculum based upon
  consequential human experiences common to all people;
- Third, the high school should prepare all students for work and
  further education through a program of electives that develop
  individual aptitudes and interests; and
- Fourth, the high school should help all students fulfill their
  social and civic obligations through school and community
  service. (pp. 66–7)

Part III, 'What Every Student Should Learn', reviews programs at
High School's field sites. Among the topics discussed are how students
decide what courses they should or shouldn't take, how programs are
organized and structured, and what student's actual course transcripts
reveal about their learning. There are two observations in this section:
high school studies are badly fragmented and few consistent national
patterns emerge; and students frequently 'shopped around' for their
courses, and in the end, took fewer academic subjects than did their
predecessors. *High School* maintains that substance, not time, is the
urgent problem in high school education. It lays out a 'Core of
Common Learning' as the cohesive curriculum base which all high
school students ought to pursue (see Figure 3). This core curriculum

Figure 3:   *Proposed Core of Common Learning: High School* (1983, p. 177.)

	Academic units
Language, 5 units	
Basic English: Writing	1
Speech	½
Literature	1
Foreign Language	2
Arts	½
History, 2½ units	
U.S. History	1
Western Civilization	1
Non-Western Studies	½
Civics, 1 unit	1
Science, 2 units	
Physical science	1
Biological science	1
Mathematics	2
Technology	½
Health	½
Seminar on work	½
Senior Independent Project	½
TOTAL	14½

consists of 14½ Carnegie units per semester, or appropriately one-half to two-thirds of the credits generally required for high school graduation.

The core of common learning is designed for students who must live in an interdependent complex world. Upon graduation, students are supposed to have the 'ability to bring together information from ideas across the disciplines, organize their thoughts, reach conclusions, and, in the end, use knowledge wisely' (p. 117). The English language is the cornerstone of learning at both elementary and secondary levels. It is the use of complex symbol systems that separates human beings from all other forms of life, the report asserts. As students study language and 'become proficient in self-expression, the quality of their thinking also will improve' (p. 85). Language study comprises several different kinds of courses (writing, speech, literature, foreign language and the arts), all of which are carefully monitored to make sure that no student falls behind. The importance of motivating youngsters in their language studies is emphasized by Herminia Uresti, an elementary school principal in a Hispanic area of Houston:

> When asked how she accounted for student progress, Ms. Uresti said she had no magic formula, 'we simply expect that every child can perform, and they do. It is very important to have high expectations. Many think that because children come

from impoverished homes they have no intellectual abilities. That is simply not the case'. (p. 87)

Similarly, students would be taught to evaluate what they hear, 'to understand how ideas can be clarified or distorted, and to explore how the accuracy and reliability of an oral message can be tested' (pp. 92–3). In the end, suggests *High School*, understanding is the whole purpose of language study. Says one University of Chicago professor, 'We practice a rhetoric of inquiry' (p. 93).

Courses in literature, foreign language, history, western civilization, non-western studies, and the arts are included in the core of common learning because of their relationship to 'cultural literacy' and human understanding on both an interpersonal and global level. A year's study of civics focuses on the traditions of democratic thought, governmental structures, and contemporary political and social issues. Again, the emphasis is on students' active pursuit of learning; civic literacy must be based on what citizens know and not 'blind belief in one or another set of professed experts' (p. 105). To this end, *High School* encourages actual community participation and first-hand experience in political events.

In science education, *High School* proposes a two-year sequence of basic courses in biological and physical sciences. 'These courses should be taught in a way that gives students an understanding of the principles of science that transcend the disciplines' (p. 107), in other words, through an interdisciplinary approach to the meaning of science and the scientific process. Advanced courses in science (biology, chemistry, and physics) would be available for students pursuing further study and eventual professional preparation.

The core of common learning contains a two-year mathematics sequence at the high school level. Students coming into that sequence 'should be able to add, subtract, multiply, and divide; and, in a larger sense, they should understand the problem-solving process' (p. 108). *High School* proposes a formal assessment of students' mathematics proficiency the year before they enter high school in order to identify those students who need remediation at the earliest possible time.

In addition to these more traditional courses, the core curriculum contains four innovative requirements. Three of these, a half-year course on technology, a course on health and a seminar on work complement the adolescent's transition to adulthood. The fourth course is 'a new Carnegie unit' made up of a Senior Independent Project in which students, under faculty supervision, work on community service projects. In some ways, this last requirement is Boyer's way of linking curriculum to Deweyian philosophy and the education of the whole child.

Finally, *High School* addresses the significance of work and lifelong learning and their relevance to the core of common learning. It reviews the role of vocational programs in the high school curriculum and comes up with a relatively negative assessment, especially for programs serving male students:

> There is . . . essentially no difference in employment advantages between male graduates of high school trade, industry, and business programs, on the one hand, and male general education graduates on the other. (p. 121)

Female students in secretarial work fare somewhat better initially, but, according to *High School*, over time, the differences between students in business programs and those in general education blur. The rapid change in both office equipment and job requirements plays against the long-term relevance of many commercial education programs. Vocational education's most telling defect is, however, that 'vocational students are often academically short-changed. Job training is being acquired at the high cost of a quality education . . . options for the future are restricted' (p. 123).

High School depicts vocational education as being part of the same low expectations syndrome that occurs in schools with large populations of disadvantaged children. The vocational program is where to send less gifted students 'who are able to work with their hands rather than their heads' (p. 124). The report cites similar findings in John Goodlad's *A Study of Schooling*, where students in low tracks are exposed to far less challenging material, less effective instructional practices, and low level cognitive processes. The real problem for educators, according to *High School* is to figure out how to instruct these children in the core curriculum so as to maximize their academic success. Ultimately, the report calls for the elimination of the multiple track curriculum because of its insidious and divisive effect on students. 'Students are divided between those who think and those who work, when, in fact, life for all of us is a blend of both' (p. 126). The one-track system, built on the common core of learning, would offer a cluster of electives from which students could choose either vocational training or more academics. The entire curriculum would be accompanied by an appropriate assessment program and a better system for following-up on graduates than is available today.

Part IV, 'The Heart of the Matter', focuses on the role of the teacher in the secondary school program. Inevitably, this discussion also involves the student's role in the instructional process. Two themes emerge: teachers are frustrated by the inadequate structure of the educational system, and students are often bored by emphasis on content coverage and the paucity of meaning in their studies. This double dilemma becomes plain in an analysis of teacher and student roles:

Teachers

- Teachers have too many students and too little class time free of trivia tasks;
- Teachers participate very limitedly in the decisions about the organization or pedagogy in the instructional process;
- Teachers compromise on assignment rigor rather than face uncooperative students; and
- Teachers are confused over both the standards and the goals of education and how these translate to everyday instruction; there is little consistency with respect to high expectations for all students.

Students

- Student's concentration on textbook material robs them of the richness and excitement of original works;
- Students suffer from information overload and little real challenge to participate or make decisions about their own education; and
- Students are rarely exposed to a variety of instructional methods that range from lecturing to questioning in a Socratic style.

Boyer refers positively to Adler's analysis in the *Paideia Proposal* in which different modes of teaching are geared to the ways in which students learn. He also points to Goodlad's study to confirm the relationship between higher order reasoning tasks and sophisticated learning. Boyer's model teacher is one who is both intellectually demanding and relates to students with the sensitivity and warmth of a trusted friend.

High School contends that major adjustments in the teaching profession will be necessary before sound instruction is possible: high school teachers should have no more than four class meetings per day, plus one seminar period for helping students with independent projects; every teacher should have a minimum of 60 minutes class preparation time per day; and teachers should be exempt from routine monitoring of halls and lunchrooms. Similarly, the intellectual climate of the school should be stimulated by rewarding creative teaching ideas, establishing a Teacher Excellence Fund, and maintaining a safe school. The report also touches briefly on the need to improve the image of the teacher in the larger community — to enhance respect for teachers and reward success with recognition. An extensive discussion focuses on the need to improve teachers' salaries, the importance of scholarship incentives in recruiting better students for teaching careers, and the need to improve teacher education programs. *High School* recommends that all teachers have a liberal arts base, a 'B' grade average or better, a major in an academic discipline, and a master's degree in education. The content of the fifth-year program includes four professional career courses: Schooling in America, Learning Theory and Research, Teaching of Writing and The Use of Technology, along with class-room observation and teaching experience. One further feature is a seminar program with outstanding scholar-teachers that concentrates on inter-disciplinary themes in the core curriculum. Teachers would be certified at the conclusion of the fifth year. Once certified, they would be on a career ladder with varying status levels keyed to performance and salary. The report goes on to support the notion of hiring part-time instructors from business and industry to alleviate teacher shortages and provide course enrichment.

High School devotes a chapter to technology in the teaching profession. It reviews various media breakthroughs of the past quarter century and hails the advent of micro-processors as both a challenge and an opportunity for instructional creativity. That significant software to serve the core of common learning has not been developed, the report remarks, is largely because the full implications of what computers and related media mean to learning and knowledge acquisition are not understood. The remedy to this is a collaboration between computer manufacturers and schools.

In Part V, 'A School that Works', *High School* turns to the principal's leadership role. Principals should have the same basic classroom preparation and experience as teachers, the report says, but in addition, they must be skilled managers. There is little sympathy with excesses of administrative bureaucracy. Like teachers, principals need to improve the status of their profession, and one way to do this is by returning to them authority over hiring and budget. In short, *High School* envisions that the impetus to rebuild excellence in education will come from the creative abilities of independent building leaders.

High School also stresses the need for more personalized education — smaller schools and classes with more opportunities for all students to participate — and cites relevant research on the effects of such arrangements. Students with special needs — gifted as well as high-risk students — are more likely to get the special attention they need in schools where the individual counts. For society's sake as well as for the student's benefit, alternative programs should be established to help these marginal students. Such programs probably need to begin in the elementary school. The chapter closes by challenging the National Commission on Excellence in Education's position on the amount of time students spend in school.

> The urgent need is not lengthening the school day or school year, but using more effectively the time schools already have — more time to complete a science laboratory experiment, more time to write essays and critique them, more time to engage in extended foreign language conversation. (p. 232)

Part VI, 'Connections Beyond the School', focuses on the world beyond school — on higher education, the business world, and public commitment. Articulating secondary schooling with higher education, coordinating goals on academic standards throughout the system, placing able high school students in college-level courses, and retraining and enriching school staffs are all mentioned as areas in need of improvement.

Finally, *High School* examines public commitment to education, something which it differentiates from trust (or lack thereof) in schools. It asserts that the federal role is no less important in education than it is in health, welfare or national defense. Nonetheless, it calls on local coalitions of citizens to lead the push for change. The report concludes with a rallying cry:

> The success or failure of the American high school will determine the quality of our democracy, the strength of our economy, the security of our defense, and the promise of our ideals. The time has come for America to stand behind its belief in public education. (p. 297)

Academic Preparation for College: What Students Need to Know and Be Able to Do

Academic Preparation for College is the major agenda of the Educational Equality Project of the College Board. Issued in 1983, the forty-six-page document represents agreement among several committees of educators on what students need to know and do in order to succeed in college. It presents not so much a national curriculum, as a preferred pattern of academic preparation for all students who plan to enter college. The College Board maintains that the pattern is also useful for students going directly into the world of work. Equity is, in fact, one of the report's major foci.

Academic Preparation for College is structured around Basic Academic Competencies and Basic Academic Subjects. Competencies are 'the broad intellectual skills essential to effective work in all fields of college study' (*Academic Preparation for College*, 1983, p. 7). These skills cut across knowledge disciplines and are not specific to any particular discipline. They are 'developed abilities, the outcomes of learning and intellectual discourse' (p. 7), and, as such, are tied to levels of accomplishment that can be measured. There are seven competency areas, the last one added after considerable debate among the members of the committee:

- Reading
- Writing
- Speaking and Listening
- Mathematics
- Reasoning
- Studying and
- Observing.

Competencies are described according to specific abilities. For example:

(Reading) 'The ability to vary one's reading speed and method (survey, skim, review, question, and master) according to the type of material and one's purpose for reading' (p. 7).

(Reasoning) 'The ability to draw reasonable conclusions from information found in various sources, whether written, spoken, or displayed in tables and graphs, and to defend one's conclusions rationally' (p. 10).

(Observing) 'The ability to use different levels of observing (for example, general overview, detailed observation, intense inspection), to recognize the distinctive features of observed phenomena, and to relate such observations to broader patterns and generalities'. (p. 36)

The reason for spelling out competencies in this manner is to help schools and students know exactly what is expected of them and to set effectiveness criteria for school programs.

Along with seven competencies, *Academic Preparation for College* proposes six Basic Academic Subjects for college entrants:

- English
- The Arts
- Mathematics
- Science
- Social Studies and
- Foreign Language.

The report introduces each subject by an explanation of *why* this area is important for college. A second section outlines *what* students need to know and be able to do in a particular subject. This latter discussion generally elaborates on the competencies or suggests additional learning outcomes in the given area. Competencies in English, for example, include reading and literature, writing, and speaking and listening; mathematics competencies include computing, statistics, algebra, geometry, and functions.

A third section of *Academic Preparation for College* argues that there is 'an emergency need' for computer competency. Students entering college should understand what computers are, how they work, and how they influence the study of academic disciplines. For some students, knowledge of computing is essential, among them those who are planning science or engineering careers.

The College Board concedes that aspects of its program need fine tuning. It leaves teachers and administrators to determine curricular and instructional approaches that can achieve desired outcomes, and advises only that 'students will achieve these learning outcomes most readily when instruction is keyed to the stages of development' (p. 32). It warns, however, that upgrading writing, reading, reasoning, and other competencies will probably change the current school program and the instructional environment, and may involve personnel usually not included in direct instruction, guidance counselors for example.

Finally, *Academic Preparation for College* exhorts school boards and institutions of higher education to help make the proposed competencies a reality.

Action for Excellence: A Comprehensive Plan to Improve Our Nation's Schools

Action for Excellence is a report of the Task Force on Education for Economic Growth of the Education Commission of the States. Co-chaired by a corporate executive and two state governors, the Task Force reflects the interests of business leaders, eleven state governors, state legislators, and various educators or educational association leaders. The report is marked 'urgent' and calls for both local and national action to help schools better serve the needs of the American workplace.

The goal of *Action for Excellence* is to improve students' performance in school and, ultimately, in the workplace. The means for doing this is 'mastery of higher order skills' (*Action for Excellence*, 1983, p. 9) — skills that go beyond the basics, those associated with technological development. Concerned too, for example, with issues like unemployment and obsolescence, the report emphasizes 'learning to learn new abilities', being flexible in making new applications, and using technology creatively. Its authors see the main purpose of schooling as imparting analysis, problem solving, reasoning, and conceptualizing skills to meet the demands of a complex global environment.

Action for Excellence seeks to reorganize the educational system so that it can devote itself to its prime task. The report makes the following recommendations to correct what is sees as dysfunctional relationships that are doing the system more harm than good:

- Develop state and local plans of action K–12 to address needs cited by the Task Force;
- Create partnerships among business, labor, and education to make educational improvement a community concern;
- Marshal existing and additional resources to help improve education;
- Improve the status and regard for the teaching profession through higher pay, better inservice, and greater participation;
- Make the academic experience more demanding, strengthen the curriculum, and increase actual instructional time;

- Provide quality assurance through better assessment, stricter certification, and periodic testing of agreed-upon skills and consistently train and recruit for similar abilities;
- Improve leadership and management in the schools; and
- Serve all the students in the population, in particular those who are unserved or underserved such as women and minorities, academically gifted, absentees, handicapped, and dropouts.

Action for Excellence shows serious concern about science and mathematics achievement, and schools' ability to adapt to technology. American education has only begun to scratch the surface in integrating modern technology into instructional programs, it remarks. It then compares American schools with those in Japan, the Soviet Union, and other industrialized countries and cites recent NAEP scores, noting particularly the drop in students' higher order skill performance. One reason for these falling scores, according to the report, is the seeming lesser exposure of young students to science and mathematics. It also laments the lack of summer training institutes for teachers, such as were held in the past, and the paucity of current curriculum revision efforts.

Action for Excellence calls for state and local response to the problems of schools. Its authors hold implicit faith in grass roots efforts to free education of 'caste and class' (p. 43). It admits that the task is a sober challenge, but assures the reader that the American people can and will meet the challenge successfully. Economic growth, observes the report, is not merely a utilitarian goal but an enabling task that will bring fulfillment to the culture as a whole.

Appended to the report is a list of competencies similar to those presented in the College Board's *Academic Preparation for College*. In fact, the College Board's list is noted as its base. However, *Action for Excellence* proposes four additional competency areas. These are scientific, basic employment, economic and computer literacy competencies. Consistent with its emphasis on knowledge for success in the workplace, the report suggests that some of the practical skills needed for academic learning are the same as those required by a good worker. With these competencies in place, the writers believe 'we can foster a great renewal and invigoration of our education for the twenty-first century' (p. 50).

Making the Grade: Report of the Twentieth Century Fund Task Force on Federal Elementary and Secondary Education Policy

Making the Grade is the report of the Twentieth Century Fund Task Force on Federal Elementary and Secondary Education Policy. The Twentieth Century Fund, which dates from 1919, is an independent research foundation that undertakes economic, political, and social policy studies. Members of the Task Force include prominent leaders from higher education and public school administration.

There is one overarching message in the Twentieth Century Fund's Report: educational improvement is a preeminently *national* need. *Making the Grade* is future oriented; although it examines past practices and policies, its focus is on the requisites of an advancing technological world. It acknowledges that elementary and secondary schools have not met the nation's educational expectations, but it does not dwell on blame. Rather, it seeks to uncover those particular problems that keep the country from ensuring 'the availability of large numbers of skilled and capable individuals without whom we cannot sustain a complex and competitive economy' (*Making the Grade*, 1983. p. 3). The national challenge, the report indicates, is to switch the focus from regulations and mandates to incentives.

The problems that *Making the Grade* addresses generally fall into three categories: quality, equality, and quality control. Like many of the other reports, the Twentieth Century Fund document recognizes America's uniqueness in seeking quality education for all its students. What is needed, it proposes, is a 'reasonable and effective balance between quality and equality' (p. 7), and the collaboration of lay citizens with professional educators.

Quality issues touch four areas: teaching, proficiency in English, fluency in a foreign language, and proficiency in mathematics and science — areas keenly associated with competitive, industrialized economies. *Making the Grade* calls for the establishment of a national Master Teachers Program and plays down the role of labor unions. In identifying the educated citizen of a technological age, it sets a standard for all public education students:

> We recommend, then, that students in elementary school learn to read, write, speak, and listen in English. As children advance in grade, these skills should be continually improved. By the time they finish high school, students ought to possess such

advanced cognitive skills as reasoning, critical analysis, the ability to explain and understand complex ideas, and to write clearly and correctly. (p. 11)

Making the Grade acknowledges that these are new demands on education. Higher order skills, for example, were once important for only a few in the United States, but today's competitive world permits not even the slightest slack. These are now the skills that all students should possess. But, says the report, complying with these new demands requires a continued federal role in education. Leadership in education is no less important than 'national leadership in health, agriculture, the physical sciences, and weaponry' (p. 18).

Changing American demographics, says the report, have created several problems of equity: increased numbers of students underskilled in English, fewer students able to speak a second language fluently, and students not having mastered specialized subjects such as mathematics and science. To remedy these failings, *Making the Grade* proposes that:

- The federal government clearly state that the most important objective of elementary and secondary education in the United States is the development of literacy in the English language;
- Federal funds now going to bilingual programs be used to teach non-English speaking children how to speak, read, and write English;
- Every American public school student [should] have the opportunity to acquire proficiency in a second language; and
- The federal government [should] emphasize programs to develop basic scientific literacy among all citizens and to provide advanced training in science and mathematics for secondary school students.

Another recommendation of the report is that the federal government extend 'impact aid' to school populations of grave need such as special education and handicapped students, immigrant children, and particularly impoverished groups. Although the report takes a negative view of tax credit plans and tuition vouchers, it calls for special federal attention to students with extensive remediation needs:

The Task Force recommends the establishment of special federal fellowships for them, which would be awarded to school districts to encourage the creation of small, individualized programs staffed by certified teachers and run as small-scale academies. (p. 20)

These academies would provide personalized, private-like education in the kind of supportive environments some public school students need to survive the system. Task Force members, however, did not all agree with this proposal; one member wanted similar specialized treatment for the most able students and another feared such a program would lead to a new form of school segregation.

Making the Grade also notes the unique importance of educational research as a responsibility of the US Department of Education. It mentions pursuits such as information gathering, data research, and especially the reporting of student performance nation-wide as being particularly appropriate federal tasks. Another area deemed to be federal responsibility is fundamental research — research that goes beyond relatively useless 'quick fix' efforts — into the learning process.

> The more that is known about how youngsters learn, the better they can be taught. Learning is an immensely complicated affair, and progress has been made on it in recent years, partly with federal support. But the federal government spends a pittance on such research compared with its support for basic research into health, agriculture, the physical sciences, and weaponry. More money is needed, enough to enlist able scholars in the process — as designers of research agendas, as researchers, as 'peer reviewers' of research proposals, and as evaluators of research findings. (pp. 18–19)

The report suggests further that the effectiveness of specific federally-funded programs be made common public knowledge.

Finally, *Making the Grade* entreats state and local governments to strengthen teaching in those curricular areas where the problems are greatest. It favors no one school curriculum or teacher education program, but does promote offering all young people the most rigorous educational experience possible. The cost of such an effort, says *Making the Grade*, is an essential investment if this country expects 'to be a leader among nations in the next century' (p. 13).

Educating Americans for the 21st Century: A Plan of Action for Improving Mathematics, Science and Technology Education for all American Elementary and Secondary Students so that their Achievement is the Best in the World by 1995

Educating Americans for the 21st Century is by the National Science Board's Commission on Precollege Education in Mathematics, Science and Technology for the National Science Foundation. It is a very future-oriented report that goes beyond identifying problems to actually suggesting practical solutions to the needs of American education in the coming century. Its goal is real achievement by all American students by 1995, one school generation away.

The report revolves around one central theme: the technological world is a very complex competitive environment and all persons in it need better higher order skills and more understanding of its workings than they have developed thus far. Education must foster a new set of basics for America's citizens or the country may become an industrial dinosaur. Basics, as defined by the Science Board, focus on mathematics, science and technology:

> We must return to basics, but the 'basics' of the 21st century are not only reading, writing and arithmetic. They include communication and higher problem-solving skills, and scientific and technological literacy — the thinking tools that allow us to understand the technological world around us. (*Educating Americans for the 21st Century*, 1983, p. 5)

Throughout, the report emphasizes that excellence is not an elitist priority, and that this new agenda is for all students in America's schools. Nonetheless, it acknowledges that different students and different communities may have different program requisites. The report also distinguishes between general course preparation and professionally-oriented schooling at the secondary level.

Educating Americans for the 21st Century proposes an eight-point action plan to upgrade instruction in mathematics, science and technology. This action plan includes:

- Building a strong and lasting national commitment to quality mathematics, science and technology education for all students;
- Providing earlier and increased exposure to these fields;

- Providing a system for measuring student achievement and participation;
- Retraining current teachers, retaining excellent teachers, and attracting new teachers of the highest quality and the strongest commitment;
- Improving the quality and usefulness of the courses that are taught;
- Establishing exemplary programs — landmarks of excellence — in every community to foster a new standard of academic excellence;
- Utilizing all available resources, including new information technologies and informal education; and
- Establishing a procedure to determine the costs of required improvements and how to pay for them. (p. vi)

Specific recommendations seek to make each of these steps a reality. Networking among various interest groups, for example, is one way to raise community awareness of the need for better mathematics, science and technology instruction. Communities and school districts would also form partnerships with business and academia. At the federal and state levels, councils would be established to address the new basics. Additional linkages would join the National Science Foundation and research and development projects with classroom teachers, curriculum developers, cognitive psychologists, scientists and industrial experts. Right now, says the report, science and mathematics education are often misperceived as being somewhere between *Star Wars* and *Dr. Who*. The real needs in these areas are not well understood by the larger society. What is even more unfortunate, however, is that this attitude on the part of adults has infected the children themselves:

> There are children who have had little experience with tools and toys that develop problem-solving and manipulative skills, who have had little guided experience with physical and biological phenomena that are all around them, and who believe that science is extremely difficult and that scientists are strange people. (p. 59)

Obviously, 'such children are poor candidates for mathematics or science in the classroom' (p. 59).

A second tactic in the Science Board's plan is to retrain teachers. The report does not downplay the need to attract more able candidates to teaching; nor does it ignore poor teaching conditions and pay scales.

These things alone, however, are unlikely to improve the quality of instruction — and that, says the report, is the crux of the matter. Current staff need more inservice preparation and summer institutes; university preparation programs should have higher standards for the certification of future teachers. The ability to instruct effectively is viewed as absolutely essential for reaching a student population with serious deficits. 'The Commission found ... that when [these students] are exposed to a good learning environment, these students perform as well as any. Low achievement norms do not reflect ability; they reflect a lack of preparation and early exposure' (p. 13). Moreover, *Educating Americans for the 21st Century* uses Torsten Husén's data to compare American education to education in other industrial societies, and concludes that expectations for lesser achieving students are too low. Better motivation and more concerted qualitative instruction and materials can improve the situation, says the report, but better teachers are the key ingredient.

Closely allied with the need for better instruction is the need for an improved course of study. *Educating Americans for the 21st Century* deals extensively with the question of what should be taught and how. It notes that mathematics and science instruction have some very specific goals in the educational system:

> ... to promote independent thought and judgment, analytic capacity, and the maximum development of each individual's potential. American scientists and mathematicians excel in theoretical and experimental science and mathematics and gain world-wide recognition as original thinkers. (p. 21)

The report emphasizes that qualitative change can only come about by 'creating islands of excellence' (p. 24), real cooperative experiences in local settings for teachers, curriculum specialists, and district administrators. The post-industrial period presents particular needs that require many groups of educators to work together.

> These needs result from the explosion of knowledge in scientific and mathematical fields; the availability of new technologies for the communication of this knowledge, the recent results of cognitive and behavioral research about how students think and learn, and the failure of some teachers to keep their skills current. (p. 41)

Educating Americans for the 21st Century does not anticipate a singular curriculum for all students, but it does expect a revamping of

current educational programs so that practical skill development under-
lies the entire course of study. Society, it maintains, needs problem
solvers not technicians. The redesign of science and mathematics
curricula is envisioned in terms of a new set of educational objectives:

> The introduction of practical problems which require the
> collection of data, the communication of results and ideas and
> the formulation and testing of solutions or improvements
> would:
>
> 1 improve the use and understanding of calculation and
>   mathematical analysis;
> 2 sharpen the student's ability to communicate verbally and to
>   write precisely;
> 3 develop problem-solving skills;
> 4 impart scientific concepts and facts that can be related to
>   practical applications;
> 5 develop a respect for science and technology and more
>   generally for quantitative observation and thinking; and
> 6 stimulate an interest in many to enter scientific, engineering
>   and technical careers. (p. 45)

In computer technology in particular, hands-on experience is viewed as
critical. The report recommends that all students become familiar with
computers and how they work as part of their general education.
Students who show 'a special interest in and ability for computing' (p.
100) should have the opportunity to pursue advanced training and
career preparation.

The report also contains specific requirements for mathematics and
science for study at both the elementary and secondary levels. It calls
for a minimum of 60 minutes per day of mathematics and 30 minutes
per day of science in grades K-6, and a full year's course of both
mathematics and science in grades 7 and 8. In high school, all students
would take at least three years of mathematics, including one year of
algebra, and three years of science and technology, with one semester
devoted to computer science. Moreover, all secondary schools would
offer advanced mathematics and science courses. The urgency for these
courses is such that the report strongly advises they be in place by the
fall of 1985.

Included in the recommendations are course topics and criteria for
selecting new curricula. Course guidelines are presented developmen-

tally with examples given at the elementary as well as the secondary level. Operationally-oriented outcomes in thinking and cognitive skills are keyed to each developmental age. For example:

- (Elementary mathematics) Understanding of arithmetic operations and knowledge of when and where specific operations should be used;
- Instruction for students in *grades 7 and 8* should place emphasis on the biological, chemical and physical aspects related to the personal needs of adolescents; and to the development of qualitative analytical skills. Instruction at this level should continue to build on student's earlier experiences and be designed to achieve ... outcomes through experimentation, text and community resources; and
- (High School Physics) Laboratory experiences including opportunities to acquire information inductively.

There is an underlying assumption in this educational approach that learning follows 'the natural curiosity of children' (p. 97) and that effective instruction is built upon a young child's 'innate' sense of subject matter. Similarly, there is a presumption that the earlier new technologies are introduced to youngsters, the better the chances for successful instruction.

Educating Americans for the 21st Century cites a litany of problems that need to be resolved before curricula can be modified. One question is how to integrate courses; for example, how to connect geometry to junior high studies of algebra. Other questions concern interdisciplinary relationships and how to introduce computers and technology into more traditional subject matter.

The report points out that although local efforts can significantly raise awareness and interest in technology, other challenges of technology require more than a grass roots effort. It asks the National Science Foundation to take a leadership role in evaluating developments in the new information technologies and maintaining an information exchange with the professional community. Linkages through the national councils mentioned earlier are also encouraged, as are contacts with state and regional teacher education and computer centers. Another major activity of the National Science Foundation should be to spearhead research, particularly to 'further the recent progress in the cognitive sciences, and ... investigate integration of educational technologies into the processes of teaching and learning' (p. 48). A further recommendation is that both basic studies and classroom application of this research be supported by federal funds.

Educating Americans for the 21st Century goes on to examine the potential impact of informal or experiential learning. The power of visual media, the influence of television broadcasting, and collaborative community activities are all regarded as supplements which can 'reinforce the lessons of the classroom and lend meaning and relevance to the rigor and discipline of formal study' (p. 59). There is a spirit of life-long learning and total community involvement assumed in this report. The report's authors want all citizens to be aware of opportunities to experience science in the real-world laboratory of the natural community. Equally important is the assumption that the purpose of knowledge about mathematics, science and technology is to serve 'national and global welfare' (p. 98).

Last but certainly not least, *Educating Americans for the 21st Century* discusses the financial implications of supporting educational improvement. One necessary cost is the sharing of exemplary efforts with school officials across the country; another is overseeing national assessment and stimulating teacher training programs. The report keys specific recommendations to costs as well as to the agency or level of organization designated as the most appropriate for a particular task. It also outlines and analyzes the effect on the federal budget. Approximately $1.51 billion is proposed for the first year of the program and about $1 billion per year over the next five years. In terms of the relationship between cost and school improvement, *Educating Americans for the 21st Century* takes a confident and positive stand:

> Americans will accept added costs if they are convinced that the money is being spent wisely, fairly, and efficiently, if the blueprint for improvement is clear, and if they begin to see significant results within a reasonable period of time. (p. 7)

The National Science Board's Commission on Precollege Education in Mathematics, Science and Technology believes its report is such a blueprint.

Horace's Compromise: The Dilemma of the American High School

Horace's Compromise by Theodore R. Sizer is the first of three volumes anticipated from *A Study of High Schools*, a five-year research project co-sponsored by the National Association of Secondary School Principals (NASSP) and the Commission on Educational Issues of the National Association of Independent Schools (NAIS). Sizer, now at Brown University, is an American historian and former Dean of Harvard's Graduate School of Education as well as a former Headmaster at Phillips Academy. As Chairman of *A Study of High Schools*, Sizer worked with twelve researchers who observed fifteen cooperating high schools. In the course of his research, Sizer himself visited numerous public and private schools in this country and abroad, and reviewed current and historic literature related to teaching and learning in high schools. *Horace's Compromise* was published early in 1984. The book is premised on the theory that a detailed understanding of the past is an essential component of effective reform. Like Mortimer Adler and Ernest Boyer, Theodore Sizer is a member of the Paideia Group.

Horace's Compromise is divided into four sections: The Students, The Program, The Teachers, and The Structure. The prologue reveals the compromise that exemplary, but fictional, high school English teacher, Horace Smith, has 'realistically' adopted: Smith doesn't fight the system; instead of assigning what he should to his 120 students, Smith demands only what he and they can conveniently cope with. After school, he goes to a second job at his brother-in-law's liquor store. The actors in this study are portrayed through a series of vignettes, each described with a novelist's penchant for detail. Vignettes are followed by criticism and recommendations for what the relationships between characters ought to be if schools are to become effective and productive institutions.

The report discusses extensively the roles of teachers and students in American high schools. The interplay of the teacher and the taught, the unique relationship of instruction and learning, and the specific exploration of knowledge and knowing are the essential elements of schooling as Sizer sees them. He focuses on adolescence because this vulnerable period is pivotal in many of life's eventual outcomes. Teachers, during this period, can play a key role in teenagers' academic, moral and social development if they are committed and willing to accept difficult educational tasks. By and large, notes *Horace's Compromise*, American educators are not up to doing so and, unfortunately, some don't want to.

What are high schools for? *Horace's Compromise* maintains their primary goal should be to help adolescents use their minds well, to think clearly and imaginatively, and to be well-informed. Teachers are central in this process ...

> ... not merely to subject the pupils to brute training ... but to
> develop their powers of thought, of taste, of judgment. High
> schools exist to help them with these uses of their minds. (p. 4)

In the triangle of teacher-student-subject area, the relationship between
the teacher and the student is the driving force behind schooling.
'Learning is a humane process, and young humans look to those elders
with whom they are in daily contact for standards, for help, and as
models' (p. 4), the report states. It should go without saying then that
schooling's most important processes take place in the classroom.
Unfortunately, Sizer and his staff found much amiss in the classrooms
of America's high schools.

Another question that arises in *Horace's Compromise* is the honesty
of the educational process. Do teachers clearly understand their obliga-
tion to students in achieving the goals of secondary education?

> High schools must respect adolescents more and patronize them
> less. The best respect is high expectations for them, and a level
> of accountability more adult in its demand than childlike. We
> should expect them to learn more while being taught less. Their
> personal engagement with their own learning is crucial; adults
> cannot 'give' them an education. Too much giving breeds
> docility, and the docility of students' minds is a widespread
> reality in American high schools. (p. 34)

A related question is whether education truly serves the diversity of
young people in our schools. The report sharply rebukes secondary
schools for using a rigid and impersonal three-track instructional
system to subtly reinforce social class differences. Entitled, wealthier
students living in the suburbs have perhaps twice the educational
resources of the poor; vocational programs are often nothing more than
a 'cruel social dumping ground' (pp. 35–6). The truth of the system
catches up when these students graduate from high school — if, in fact,
they stay in school that long — poorly prepared for work and with no
plans to further their education. Much of this the report blames
on education's propensity of putting people and things into neat
bureaucratic categories, shoving aside the marvelous idiosyncratic
differences among various human beings. Good teachers are those who
can rise above this and break through the bureaucracy to address the
needs of a heterogeneous population in imaginative ways.

> Accordingly, good teachers take note of these easy generalities,
> and then, freeing themselves as much as possible from the trap
> of stereotyping, deal with each student as an individual. (p. 39)

Horace's Compromise stresses the value of motivation in the teaching-learning process. On several occasions, it uses the metaphor of 'the hungry student', an inquisitive youngster eager to learn and ready to take initiative in teaching him or herself. Inspiring such behavior is the main task of teaching and should serve as the measure of any professional incentive or reward structure. Unfortunately, Sizer and his researchers found students in American schools largely passive, relatively happy in their orderly buildings, 'but intellectually dull' (p. 56). This lack of inspiration is mirrored by mental blandness and failure to equate achievement with personally owned skills and abilities. Referring to the students' profile on the National Assessment of Educational Progress, *Horace's Compromise* comments:

> What is especially troubling is the low level of their reasoning skills, the abilities of analysis and synthesis. While students seem to be improving in rote-level, concrete learnings — vocabulary recognition and, in mathematics, simple addition, for example — their ability to think critically and resourcefully is lamentably weak and is continuing to weaken. (p. 58)

Still another change proposed by the report is in the granting of high school diplomas. These, it says, should be awarded on the basis of agreed-on mastery of academic tasks, with students fully understanding that expectations for their success are high. Moreover, the report recommends that assessments be created that permit students to show their accomplishments. It speculates that as test scores rise, so will student self-esteem.

With regard to the high school program, *Horace's Compromise* finds secondary education a fragmented assemblage of courses held together by the building's clock. The organizing structure is rigid, frighteningly uniform, and resistant to change. The amount of content covered is a key variable in what is commonly referred to as 'good teaching', yet what racing through content really does is make students 'take subjects', not participate in learning that is in any way meaningful. The report claims that attending high school has become an empty ritual for far too many students, and the high school's only purpose has become to keep thousands of teenagers generally safe and off the streets, conveniently removed from the adult labor market.

Horace's Compromise forecasts that high school at the end of the twentieth century will be vastly different from the public 'people's colleges' originally envisioned. Education's role is no longer purveying information but rather helping people use the plethora of knowledge now available. The report raises the age-old question of what knowledge is appropriate for the citizens of a democracy and responds with three basic skills — literacy, numeracy, and civic understanding. It suggests that these competencies might be appropriate goals for elementary studies, and when they are mastered compulsory attendance should cease. Attending high school should be the student's own choice.

Sizer advises that high school learning focus on ten essential skills, which are not unlike the spheres of learning in Adler's *The Paideia Proposal*. These skills include reading, writing, speaking, listening, measuring, estimating, calculating, imagining, and reasoning. He takes the position that although people are likely to learn these skills from everyday experience, schools can help young people perform them efficiently. Sizer further advocates writing as the central skill of learning, not because it is an end in itself but because it is the means that students can use to delve into their minds.

What is the appropriate curriculum for the high school? According to *Horace's Compromise*, it is subject matter which supports the student's learning essential skills; its materials 'should lead somewhere, in the eyes and mind of the student' (p. 111). Sizer quotes Bruner on the generativity of structured knowledge:

> ... grasping the structure of a subject is understanding it in a way that permits many other things to be related to it meaningfully. To learn structure, in short, is to learn how things are related. (p. 114, from Bruner, 1960, pp. 7 and 25)

Using Bruner's concept, *Horace's Compromise* recommends that high schools teach less — but that what they do teach be structured in an integrated coherent manner. This kind of structure gives the student a greater knowledge base and, therefore, results in more effective instruction. The report seeks 'the development of powers of discrimination and judgment (p. 116) as the major outcomes of the secondary program. While teachers' questions can help students develop such powers, *Horace's Compromise* places the bulk of the task of teaching on students themselves. The student must gain control over the development of knowledge.

Horace's Compromise does not advocate one program for all students. Every school must find its own way, the report says. Nevertheless, it does propose a model high school curriculum of four areas or large departments:

1   Inquiry and Expression

2 Mathematics and Science
3 Literature and the Arts
4 Philosophy and History (p. 132)

Sizer believes that the fewer the number of departments, the greater integration of knowledge. Presumably, teachers would discuss and coordinate the program they plan to instruct, and by doing so would actively construct the school's curricular core. *Horace's Compromise* also envisions high schools with smaller teaching units, and units that are based on what students can do rather than on strict age-grading.

In discussing teacher characteristics. *Horace's Compromise* rates 'good judgment' as the most important trait of effective instructors. It defines good judgment as the 'ability to find the appropriate recipe for engaging the attention and ultimately the minds and energies of their particular students' (p. 150). Teaching is an autonomous, personalized endeavor and in the successful classroom there is an agreement between the teacher and the students on the major task being pursued and the rules of the 'academic game'. Here is where Horace Smith's compromise comes to the fore. Horace and his students have agreed to do only as much as makes them all comfortable. Sizer sees this as a 'conspiracy of the least; the trade-off for the lack of hassle for everyone is the squandering of learning time for all' (p. 156). In contrast, motivating teachers establish lively teaching environments in their classrooms and essentially coach students to develop their own skills of learning and judgment. More important, perhaps, good schools make this teaching-learning process possible by giving teachers control of their classrooms and adequate means of instruction. The report surmises that such trust may be a significant difference between public and private secondary schooling in this country.

Underlying much of Sizer's view of the teacher is his assumption that teaching is a craft. Like learning, being able to instruct, according to Sizer, is a mysterious and often idiosyncratic task. It is akin to the art of acting in the theater:

> Teaching is a complex craft, one class never being quite the same as another. Treating teaching as a mere technology either reduces its goals to brute training of the children in rote skills or permits great inefficiency. Standardized high school training is wasteful. That students differ may be inconvenient, but it is inescapable. Adapting to that diversity is the inevitable price of productivity, high standards, and fairness to the students. (p. 194)

The final section of *Horace's Compromise* examines the structure of high schools, more specifically, the hierarchical bureaucracies that have developed over the last half century. Given its orientation to learners and teachers, the report finds these bureaucracies 'are today paralyzing American education. The structure is getting in the way of children's learning' (p. 206). *Horace's Compromise* speaks of the trend toward greater centralization as reducing educational practices to replicable formulas. At the same time, however, it accuses specialization of being the real villain in secondary education because it aims to achieve its own particular ends with little attention to the good of the overall institution.

Horace's Compromise insists that nothing less than a major overhaul of American secondary education will do, and that this revision should start with the needs of the developing adolescent. Reform questions should ask, 'How can adolescents be assisted in learning more efficiently?' (p. 211). The focus of the re-oriented school's program would be 'the major intellectual skills, because they are the necessary prerequisites for all useful involvement in society' (p. 212). But Sizer admits that practical matters may interfere with such a revision. A teacher, for example, probably cannot be responsible for more than eighty pupils per day if he or she is to teach meaningfully, yet in most schools such a small number of pupils per teacher is impossible. Simplifying the curriculum, or changing the school's subject matter structure so that it is not dominated by college specializations, is also likely to incur opposition, mainly because it threatens most teachers' view of what school ought to be.

In spite of these problems, however, Sizer maintains a renaissance can be generated by a few; the present is ripe for educational renewal. Recognition that student alienation is a real problem and that Horace's compromise is the wrong answer is the first step in educational change. But those in political power must make reform possible. Herein is the major dilemma of current American schooling.

Notes

1   See list of participants on each panel or commission of reviewed reports in Appendix B.
2   See list of commissioned papers noted in *A Nation at Risk* in Appendix C.

4   The Reports of the Eighties Analyzed

> No society will successfully resolve its internal conflicts if its only asset is cleverness in the management of these conflicts. It must have compelling goals that are shared by the conflicting parties; and it must have a sense of movement toward these goals.
>
> John W. Gardner, *Excellence* (1961)

The conflict and change that has characterized America's schools has drawn ample attention from social and educational chroniclers. James and Tyack (1983), for example, tie periods of school reform, both conservative and liberal, to political eras. They see the 1890s, 1950s, and 1980s as politically and economically conservative, and favoring education that emphasizes the basics, as well as a 'pulling in', 'tightening up', or 'culling down' of programs and expenditures. In contrast, in the more liberal 1930s, 1960s, and the early 1970s, Americans sought to 'broaden the functions of schooling' and 'overcome past rigidity' (p. 406).

This analysis is not unlike historian Diane Ravitch's (1983 and 1984b) interpretation of reform. Ravitch cites two major 'fashions in education', one traditional and akin to arguments advanced by the Eliot Commission in 1893 for schooling with an academic orientation; the other progressive, attracted to John Dewey's teachings and sharing *The Cardinal Principles'* faith in the individual child and education for the greater community good. Ravitch sees the current reform period as a re-emergence of 1893 mentality and expects it to continue until the pendulum swings back again. This to and fro effect, according to Ravitch, will persist until educators 'establish some sensible priorities for the kinds of things schools do' (Ravitch quoted in White, 1984, p. 17).

Dilemmas within American society are another reason for reform

(Cohen and Neufeld, 1981). Cohen and Neufeld's study of American high schools was completed prior to the writing of the current reform reports, and was influential in many of them. These two historians find a paradox between the goals of educational equality and the context of competitive American society. They conclude that 'the schools are a public institution oriented to equality in a society dominated by private institutions oriented to the market' (p. 70). Since specialized technical knowledge is now key to economic development, much of the reasoning underlying the current reform reports, say Cohen and Neufeld, hinges on goals that in reality are really confused. Reforming schools means that goals are clarified.

Michael Bakalis (1983) suggests that reform periods emerge to redefine major premises in American education: educational purpose and educational power. For there to be effective action, he says, power and purpose must combine harmoniously. Bakalis cites Americans' fear of a too-centralized-authority as a warning for educational leaders who might attempt to impose reform from 'on-high', and describes the public's faith in quality education for all, however poorly defined, as politically and economically energizing reform. Bakalis introduces the concept of efficiency for the common good as another controlling force in American education. Professional administrators made their appearance in education early in this century, much as they did in government and business. These administrators held the reins of educational power for years, but since World War II, Bakalis maintains, control has splintered among a more complex leadership. The current reforms, then, are an attempt to reestablish authority in schooling and to clarify the particular purposes of education as Americans use them today.

Three Models of Schooling

Each of the eight reform reports is rooted in specific assumptions that influence its major thrust. Sometimes, these assumptions or compelling ideas cut across several studies, creating what is, in essence, models of schooling. Three such models are borrowed here from curriculum development: content, society, and individual-driven education (Tanner and Tanner, 1975).

Content-driven schooling focuses on the subject matter of education, the courses and products associated with the disciplines of organized knowledge. Such schooling is grounded in purist traditions of international and long-range historic development and in the notion that academic pursuits lead to truth and expertise. Collective and generalized wisdom from the past constitutes knowledge and enables educators to ask questions like 'what knowledge is of most worth?' as Spencer (1963) raised the question in the middle of the nineteenth century and Broudy (1982) continues to ask today. Schools are sometimes viewed as the unique repositories of such knowledge, as well as havens for the pursuit of new information. But intellectual concentration has clearly not been a winning model in American educational history. As important as being on the cutting edge of science or a new mathematical theory may be, there is a strong proclivity toward anti-intellectualism in America's heritage.

> The current of anti-intellectualism runs deep in our history and in our society. It comprises a resentment and suspicion both of the mind itself and of those who represent it. Intellect is regarded as a form of privilege and power. It is resented as a kind of excellence, a claim to distinction, that challenges the egalitarianism of America. (Bakalis, 1983, p. 9)

Historian Richard Hofstadter (1966) traces this attitude back to the earliest conception of education in a democracy. Contrary to European goals of achieving a high culture or preserving the classics in a pure form, America's

> ... belief in mass education was not founded primarily upon a passion for the development of mind, or upon pride in learning and culture for their own sakes, but rather upon the supposed and economic benefits of education. No doubt leading scholars and educational reformers like Horace Mann did care for the intrinsic values of mind. But in trying to persuade influential men or the general public of the importance of education, they were careful to point out the possible contributions of education to public order, political democracy, or economic improvement. (p. 305)

Content-driven education has claimed a place in America's national history, but, for the most part, until the present period it has always been overshadowed by an education that values pioneering, entrepreneurship, and other more practical gains.

Society-driven schooling focuses on the common good. It is pragmatic and utilitarian, and bestows on education an important moral role. Hofstadter (1966) indicates that the historical charge of American schools was 'to form character and inculcate sound principle rather than lead to the pursuit of truth' (p. 307). In early progressivism, education was concerned with overall social needs (Radest, 1983). Although Dewey's original philosophy may later have been misinterpreted and poorly applied, its goal remained fixed on improving the quality of life and making education more useful to society (Katz, 1975). Society-driven schooling tends to see the nation as a holistic unit, the citizenry as a homogeneous body, and the mission of education as furthering the political destiny and the economic well-being of the Republic. It is no accident, according to Tyack and Hansot (1982), that

> The public school system is probably the closest Americans have come to creating an established church ... The public school represents the *only* commitment by which this society has guaranteed to look after the needs and interests of all its citizens, at least while they are young. (pp. 514–5)

Hofstader notes that in the nineteenth century 'schools were made into powerful agencies for the diffusion of social and economic opportunities' (p. 309). A school's 'worth' was always translated into 'value' associated with 'productivity' and to currency in the marketplace. By the twentieth century, schooling was prized because it enabled students to get and maintain jobs. Society was the benefactor.

Individual-driven schooling is a humanistic concept that focuses on the best and most equitable experience for the two major participants in schooling: the teacher and the student. Politically, it is linked to Jeffersonian concepts of liberty and diversity and belief in the significance of each and every individual in a democracy. The practice of universal schooling is a direct outgrowth of this philosophy. According to Freeman Butts (1979):

> The most fundamental purpose of universal schooling is the political goal of empowering the whole population to exercise the rights and cope with the responsibilities of a genuinely democratic citizenship. (p. 359)

The core of democratic citizenship consists of three elements: personal freedom, pluralism, and participatory experience. There is an assumption that an individual in pursuit of these elements must be able to make social, political, economic and personal decisions on his or her own and be responsible for the consequences of those decisions. At the heart of this conception of schooling is the belief that each citizen, barring physical or mental impairment, can acquire such decision-making capacity and desires to employ it. The experience at school — preferably a personalized one — should focus on making this happen.

There is somewhat a mixed view of the teacher in individual-driven schooling. As a citizen, the teacher shares with the student the same rights to democratic participation in the school. As an instructor, however, the teacher has not always been singled out as a uniquely endowed and valued contributor to education. To some extent, anti-intellectualism has spilled over into this view of the instructional relationship. If knowledge of subjects is little valued in the society, then teachers as instructors of subject matteer are also not very significant in the workings of the community. Hofstadter (1966) contends that students are aware of teachers' lower social status in the community and that 'American adolescents have more sympathy than admiration for their teachers' (p. 312).

There is also a strong division in American education with regard to the teacher's status at different levels of schooling. College and university teachers are 'instructors' or 'professors' and have a 'profession'; their role as content-purveyors dominates. Elementary and secondary teachers are not always depicted so positively or so independently, and their grasp of content is usually considered more modest. Sometimes only as members of an organized teachers' group does the status of these pre-collegiate teachers become significant. Shanker (1984) sees the authoritarian relationship between principals and teachers a major problem that needs attention in the current reform period. Thus, whether because of the adverse relationship between anti-intellectualism and teachers' subject matter knowledge, or because of power relationships in the school's administrative structure, individual-driven schooling, from the teacher's perspective, has a slightly tarnished history in America. Yet, the teacher as an individual — even as a cog in a bureaucratic wheel — remains a critical entity in this third model of schooling.

Each of the models of schooling reflects the policy positions and goals of certain school administrators and others in educational leadership. Consider, for example, the three models in terms of policy goals suggested by Mitchell and Encarnation (1984): quality (or excellence), efficiency, and equity. Reform periods can be analyzed by examining the models of schooling they promote relative to these goals. Similarly, the present reform reports can be analyzed by comparing their support for one or another goal. The three goals, as the three models of schooling, are not necessarily mutually exclusive. More often, educational history contains overlap, simultaneity, or combined emphasis (see Figure 4). Sorting out the relationships of the reports to the three goals may enlighten us on the underlying meaning of a particular report.

A National at Risk

A Nation at Risk is largely an efficiency-driven document. Its prime concern is the nation's welfare in a competitive world market. Education is singled out as the chief creator and preserver of the nation's prosperity, security, and civility. In arguing its utilitarian case, *A Nation at Risk* employs data-based analysis of student performance — essentially a technical interpretation of particular 'indicators' — test scores, and comparative analyses. Achievement is synonomous with test success.

As interpreted by this report, excellence has little to do with the content of schooling except as it applies to the more marketable subjects of mathematics, science, and computer technology. The curriculum that it recommends consists of the traditional English,

Figure 4: *Three Overlapping Goals of Schooling*

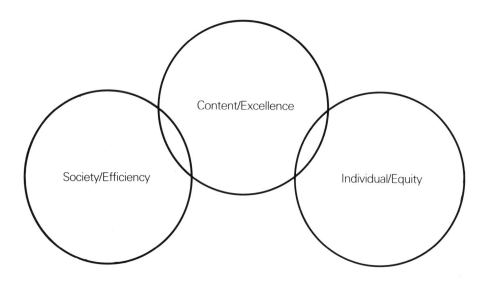

mathematics, science, and social studies, along with the 'new' basic skill of computer science. Excellence with regard to the individual learner is equated with high test performance, not achieving greater wisdom, and is assessed in terms of the learner's personal limits and abilities. In this context, learning is a specialized product or commodity rather than a general tool for further knowledge generation. Excellence in society, as depicted by *A Nation at Risk*, is realized through productivity in much the same way that a corporation becomes more cost effective by enhancing the output of its labor force. One sets standards for accomplishment and anticipates that workers will strive to meet them.

A Nation at Risk is alert to equity concerns but rarely for the well-being of individuals, as would be the case if this were an equity-driven document. The report treats youth in school as a collective national resource and considers the pluralism characteristic of American society somewhat dysfunctional when declining test scores, particularly of an increasing minority population, indicate the nation is no longer upwardly mobile. 'History is not kind to idlers' (p. 6), the report remarks and shoddy performance, it implies, cannot be tolerated. Children should strive to develop informed judgment so they can get a good job and manage their own lives. As learners, they are expected to respond to challenges, but rarely to be proactive or initiators. *A Nation at Risk* recognizes that American society is diverse, but it makes understanding diversity secondary to working for the common good. It sees the function of teaching as purveying academic substance to naive youth. Teachers are like apples in a barrel going to market. Some bad ones have crept in; neglect is causing others to go bad; and exceptional samples are in short supply.

In light of the goals underlying *A Nation at Risk*, it is not surprising that the report's recommendations are basically technical improvements. *A Nation At Risk* wants society strengthened by making greater demands of education through, for example, increased graduation standards and higher expectations of performance. It wants student performance enhanced by such procedural approaches as limiting course selection, requiring more homework, providing more teaching time, and using better textbooks and instructional materials. And, similarly, it wants an improved instructional staff by offering better working conditions and pay, and by seeking personnel from more able labor pools. *A Nation at Risk* concludes by saying it has completed its responsibility of identifying the national interest in education; it then sends the gift with the bill to the American public.

The Paideia Proposal

The Paideia Proposal is concerned with the quality of schooling as embodied in the *content* of learning, and so, essentially advocates an excellence-directed model of schooling. Strongly oriented to the great thinking of the past, the report cites education's *raison d'être* as passing this heritage from one generation to the next, and describes limitedly how this is to happen and how various people in the transfer are to be involved. The program is directed to education for individuals, and although it accepts some diversity in the population, it considers Americans much more alike than culturally different. Essentially, it believes that Americans live in a classless society.

The heart of *The Paideia Proposal* consists of three strands of knowledge. Each strand is based on a different approach to teaching and learning. The first strand involves the collected wisdom of the past, especially the liberal arts, and is to be taught primarily by telling and modelling. Content focuses on traditional, 'organized' subject areas that reflect western heritage from Greek and Roman times through to twentieth-century Europe. The instructor is the fount of all wisdom and the materials of learning are the great academic works of the past. The second strand emphasizes the development of intellectual skills. Students participate in tasks of learning and inquiry which teach them to think like the instructor. Insofar as direct exchange is vital to the process of education, *The Paideia Proposal* treats pedogogy only as an expression of the content of learning. Little is said about the instructional relationship, the dynamic exchange between the teacher and the taught. In the third strand, students explore ideas and values, largely from the past. Although students' active participation is encouraged, when Socratic questioning enters the picture, the main mode of instruction is the teacher's activity not the student's. The philosopher-king leaves little room for the individual learner in the modern groves of academe.

The Paideia Proposal develops from a premise that schooling is only part of a person's life-long education. As such, it has a narrow purpose — to develop each person's academic ability for the larger tasks of life. That ability is primarily characterized by knowing and understanding past great thinking. The report's author sees only one best route for this preparation — the single course of study for all — and discounts other alternatives as ineffective and distracting educators from their central responsibility. *The Paideia Proposal* is concerned with some equity issues, like remediation and motivation, but largely as an afterthought or only as a necessary corrective step.

The report singles out the teacher as a key figure in reform. The emphasis is not on the teacher as an individual or even as a spokesperson for democracy, although the latter is mentioned as part of the report's theoretical bases, but on a classical European view of learning that highlights the intrinsic value of education and makes the teacher the epitome of an educated person. In that regard, *Paideia* is strongly reminscent of Eliot's Committee of Ten, and about as far from *A Nation at Risk* as one can get.

High School

High School is one of the longest and probably the most comprehensive of the reform studies. Although it addresses issues of content excellence and society's efficiency, its major thesis is the development of the profession of teaching for the success of the individual teacher. That, says the report, is the 'heart of the matter' at this time of educational reform. It is a view centered on equity in schooling.

Boyer sees the role of the high school as preparing students for life as well as for work or further education. The individual's active involvement in schooling mentally, culturally, socially, and civically is key to this preparation. A 'core of common learning' provides the substance and the means for study, but is not an end of learning in and of itself. The finishing touch of high school studies is the Senior Independent Project in which every student actually uses his or her acquired knowledge in service to the community. The essence that makes learning possible, according to *High School*, is 'the centrality of language' and the ability to communicate one's ideas to one's peers and fellow citizens. Finally, *High School* equates the mastery of language with the ability to think critically. The epitome of these intellectual operations is a practicing democracy.

High School is critical of the bureaucratic complexities of modern education and recommends that teachers participate in making decisions about the education of adolescents. Bureaucracies, it notes, prevent the development of nurturing climates in which goals are personalized and realized. For example, if bureaucracies expect the achievement of minority children to be low, they convey these low expectations to teaching staffs without giving much thought to how the considerable staff resources can be used to alter the situation. Rewarding teachers' creativity and upgrading the profession in the eyes of the community are important ways to re-energize teaching and education as a whole. The report calls for principals to be instructional leaders or head teachers in the transformation of the school.

But school reform, as envisioned in *High School*, involves other players as well, particularly higher education institutions and the corporate world. A sound professional education for teachers is made up of a discipline-oriented undergraduate program and master's level graduate study focusing on teacher preparation. This advanced teacher preparation program has four parts: one is historically rooted, one is psychologically based, one emphasizes the teaching of writing, and one concentrates on the use of technology. The report does not go into depth about how or why these particular courses contribute to a teacher's professional expertise, although some of that can be inferred by its goals in the teaching/learning process. It is clear, however, that one purpose of this model of advanced preparation is to create a base for renewing respect for the profession. Individuals pursuing careers in teaching will have to commit their energies and funds to acquiring such an education; likewise, it is up to the profession to make such as high-caliber education possible. Note that it is the *voluntary* commitment of both parties that is important here, not the external requisite of an efficiency-driven model. This commitment, along with more substance in the system, is the key, according to *High School*, to professional teaching and the antidote to educational mediocrity.

Academic Preparation for College

Academic Preparation for College serves as a constitution for an efficiency or society-driven model of schooling. In one sense, it complements *A Nation at Risk* by defining standards of educational success, namely acquiring the competencies needed to go to college and being able to demonstrate them. Although concerns about what one should know are generally associated with the content-excellence model of schooling, and the report's sub-title puts content before competencies, the text actually begins with a discussion of academic competencies. Competencies are efficiency measures.

The report's authors view academic competencies as developed abilities, 'the outcomes of learning and intellectual discourse' (p. 7).

Furthermore, they propose that these competencies can be measured to determine their level of development. Of the seven competencies listed, the first four — reading, writing, speaking and listening, and mathematics — are obviously basic skills and subject to SAT assessment. Reasoning and studying are competencies of a different order and might have been discussed in terms of the courses of the curriculum, but *Academic Preparation for College* establishes only their technical importance. The inclusion of computer competency indicates the importance of technology in the school's program and is consistent with the 'new basics' advocated in *A Nation at Risk*. The conclusion of observing as a basic competency is offered as a later addition. Were the content or learning dimensions of schooling more central in *Academic Preparation for College*, the relationship of these last two competencies might have been grist for substantive discussion. As it is, however, the report only mentions them briefly and moves on rather quickly to applying them directly to specific subject matter.

Academic Preparation for College is cognizant of the need for an academic base in the nation's educational system and states several times that the opportunity to learn academic skills must be available to *every* learner. 'The promise of equal access to higher education', (p. 2) is, however, a somewhat empty promise since the report offers little detail on how the individual student can acquire the competencies needed for college entrance. The level of its discussion about schooling is very general. Similarly, although the report notes that instruction aimed at helping students acquire the competencies must be keyed to stages of intellectual development, there is no discussion of learning stages or processes or the schooling experience that might be the most beneficial at any particular time.

There is also a general acceptance in this report that it is up to teachers and administrators to translate these new standards into the everyday tasks. The report itself provides no teaching or learning strategies. It presents an efficiency model, with improved test scores as its measure of success, that depends rather heavily on teaching for the test. The notable exception, perhaps, is the admonition to students to improve their classroom attitude, attitude in this case meaning much the same as good conduct. This seems to indicate that discipline comes before wisdom or even personal satisfaction in this report's model of schooling.

There is one curious suggestion made by *Academic Preparation for College* about the role of higher eduction. This is that colleges ought to become effective remedial institutions. With this recommendation,

Academic Preparation for College strikes a decidedly different chord than *A Nation at Risk*. It may be suggesting that simply raising standards will probably not be sufficient for educational improvement; there are still individual student needs that have to be met. Some sensitivity to the problems of minority students seems in evidence here, but there is little follow-up discussion on this potentially potent idea. The introduction of observing as a competency poses another provocative topic. Efficiency-driven models of schooling most often are cut, dried, and absolute. *Academic Preparation for College* has some loose ends that hint of alternative ways of looking at schooling. The power of observation may open a host of new skills for education in the eighties. But, this area, too, is only mentioned and not developed further. One wonders whether someone will pursue these ideas more extensively in the next reform period.

Action for Excellence

Action for Excellence is another society or efficiency-driven document about schooling, but its orientation is different from either *A Nation at Risk* or *Academic Preparation for College*. First, it does not delight in reprimand but chooses instead to render a constructive critique. Second, although this report, too, focuses on academic competencies, it does not limit itself to the college-bound student but seeks to understand new skill requisites of every American citizen. *Action for Excellence* reveals a historically sensitive grasp of American culture in general and sees the current reform effort in that light. 'The challenge', it says, 'is not simply to better educate our elite, but to raise both the floor and ceiling of achievement in America' (p. 7). Equity concerns become nearly as important as society's efficiency in this study with some attention given to the content of science, mathematics, and technology instruction as well.

Action for Excellence's main message is that new world conditions demand that Americans acquire new higher order skills in order to compete in the global market. Complex skills of problem solving, reasoning, conceptualizing, and analyzing are the new criteria for an efficient and adaptable worker in the marketplace. The report implies that sophistication and intellectuality are no longer dirty words in American culture; quite conversely, they are the foundation of economic growth. The new mission of schooling, according to this report, is to develop these qualities in all American youth.

One of the report's recommendations is for Americans to arrive at a consensus about the goals of schooling. It cautions that a society marked by fragmented educational goals is obviously not going to be productive, and bids a coalition of educators, business and government leaders, and labor unions to establish the necessary consensus. Citing demographic statistics on minority urban youth, the report shows obvious deterrents to both future academic and economic growth, including poverty, unemployment, and drop-out rates. Like *A Nation At Risk*, *Action for Excellence* poses improvements such as more time-on-task and better qualified and better paid teachers as part of the solution to ailing schools, but in addition, it also suggests revising curricula and working toward both improved cognitive and motivational goals. Also like both *A Nation at Risk*, and *Academic Preparation for College*, *Action for Excellence* never really wrestles with questions such as 'how do students become better problem solvers?' or 'how do teachers instruct students to think better in complex ways?' Pedagogy is largely a non-existent concern in this report. The changes it recommends are mostly external to the actual education process and include raising certification standards, attracting better teachers, adding a little pre and in-service training for existing personnel, and putting principals in charge who can use 'effective management techniques' (p. 11). The efficiency model persists in *Action for Excellence*, even if driven by state and local coalitions and requiring more complex technical skills.

Making the Grade

Making the Grade resembles *Action for Excellence* as a society or efficiency-driven model of schooling. Although it begins with reference to the importance of citizens' ability to make wise decisions, it quickly turns to societal concerns in a complex and competitive economy. Technology and a skilled labor force are again noted as necessary ingredients for success in world markets. Recommendations in *Making the Grade* focus, in large measure, on federal initiatives — literacy programs, science and mathematics development efforts — and by doing so challenge both labor unions and proponents of bilingual education. Writers of the report view unions as associations that prevent the creation of reward systems for teachers, thereby inhibiting quality performance. Their argument with bilingual instruction is that it is keeping disadvantaged learners alienated from American society by preventing their learning English. In the main, *Making the Grade* considers literacy in the English language the chief objective of elementary and secondary education. But the purpose of such an ability is not to facilitate the learning of particular content. As in most society-efficiency reports, literacy helps forge a common nation.

Making the Grade makes two content-oriented recommendations, but these, too, are really efficiency-based. The nation needs citizens who are scientifically literate, says the report, but what is meant by scientific literacy is not stated beyond the fact citizens should be able to make intelligent political decisions about radiation, pollution, nuclear energy, and other issues. The emphasis is again pragmatic. Another recommendation deals with learning foreign languages. The report advocates giving every public school student the opportunity to acquire proficiency in a second language. The rationale for this position rests on the country's increasing involvement in competitive trade and investment with other nations. No mention is made of either science or foreign language enhancing an *individual's* intellectual capability — an equity concern. Nor is there discussion of how accomplishment in these academic areas fosters further knowledge acquisition skills — the content-excellence dimension — that might increase general scholastic aptitude.

In examining prior federal efforts at improving the nation's schools, *Making the Grade* is critical of some existing programs and laudatory of others. The report is careful to say that federal involvement in special education should continue in poor areas. It further suggests establishing new programs in concentrated immigrant communities where the local government cannot afford to do so. Although still pragmatically guided, these recommendations are sensitive to some equity interests, or at least to the residents of America's urban communities. The report also calls for two initiatives that, when compared to other reform reports, are relatively original: a strong federal role in educational research, especially in data collection, and the conduct of a fundamental study of the learning process. The language is still utilitarian, but the ideas are much more constructive than arguments proposed in *A Nation at Risk*.

The narrow focus of *Making the Grade* raises some questions about its overall arguments. Why is language literacy so central to education in a scientific and industrial age? How can areas such as English, science, and mathematics be integrated into a general curriculum? What are educators to do about the computers so highly touted in other efficiency-driven studies? Why is bilingualism a particular concern for immigrant groups today and why has America been so parochial about foreign language learning in the past? These questions may be raised in more appropriately content-excellence or individual-equity reports, but they should be broached in *Making the Grade* as well, because they are central to several of its arguments. It is disappointing that such discussion is omitted.

Educating Americans for the 21st Century

Educating Americans for the 21st Century resembles *Making the Grade* and *Action for Excellence* in several ways. It recognizes the value of forging coalitions among educators, business, and government leaders, and perceives the relationship between higher order cognitive skills and the development of science, mathematics, and technology in a complex competitive world. But the arguments presented in this report are quite different from the positions taken in society-driven documents. *Educating Americans for the 21st Century* first emphasizes content-excellence and then relates this emphasis to individual-equity goals in envisioning education for 1995.

One of this report's first assumptions is that excellence is *not* an elitist condition. Mindful of the history of the Committee of Ten, it considers owning skills and being intellectually stimulated fitting for every American youngster. Generally, says the report, both educators and the public have underestimated what can be expected of even poorly performing students. There is a natural curiosity in all children that schools need to keep alive and to develop. In the America of the future, where many more minority youngsters will seek education, schools must devise better ways to enable these students to master higher order skills — or the country's general well-being will be threatened. The report develops two major strategies to address this emergent problem: better curricula and more effective instruction.

Educating Americans for the 21st Century stresses work in mathematics, science and technology, but by no means limits itself to these content areas. Its emphasis is on practical skill improvement — something which it recognizes as developmental and integrative with all learning. The report proposes course requirements for elementary through secondary school and considers issues like types of reasoning and time requisites for learning specific subject content. *Educating Americans for the 21st Century* is mindful that learners vary, but it is also cognizant that certain times of development, such as adolescence, are particularly influential for whole groups of learners. The content to be learned, suggests the report, cannot be separated from how the individual learner both perceives and conceives it. One sees here a different accent on knowledge from the way past wisdom is treated in *The Paideia Proposal*. Teachers cannot just 'pour in' information or find it embodied in historic great works; they must take the learner into account. Moreover, the recent explosion of knowledge, especially in science, mathematics, and technology, compounds the problem of content and challenges the student to build skills to keep up with the expansion. The complex processes of thinking loom large as targets for schooling in the next century.

This report, then turns to effective instruction as the primary goal of schooling. Indeed, it dwells on pedagogy as much as *A Nation at Risk* plays up test achievement. The individual teacher and the individual student meet in the classroom; if a good learning environment exists, and there is a sound program, students will progress. The purpose of *Educating Americans for the 21st Century* is largely to make educators aware of the conditions required for this *intellectual exchange*. Like *Making the Grade*, *Educating Americans for the 21st Century* looks to cognitive science research as a means for improving instruction, especially in informing educators about the best ways to integrate technology into the learning environment. It also expects such research to add to the knowledge about the nature of problem solving among youngsters, the necessary focus of education in the new technological age. The imprint of the Nobel Laureate and cognitive scientist, Herbert Simon, is obvious in this report.

Another facet of instruction discussed in this report is the importance of actual experience in helping students and teachers understand learning in the 'new world'. Learning is not something one does just at school; the relevance of the world beyond the school to what children learn in school is a key concept in the new vision of schooling. This has implications for both students and teachers. Children need to be made aware that studies in the classroom relate to realities in the workplace, to research at universities and in business, and to the pursuits of individual scholars and scientists. Teachers need to network with other educators, to exchange information with university personnel, and with community members whose work relates to the disciplines of the classroom. *Educating Americans for the 21st Century* conceives of knowledge as a dynamic, evolving, people-related entity. Collaboration among educators is called for in an information-rich world. This viewpoint noticeably contrasts with *The Paideia Proposal* and raises serious question about the adequacy of a uniform program for all students. *Educating Americans for the 21st Century* gives a new meaning to participation in the educational establishment. It also calls for a special relationshiop between participants in education and the world of science, mathematics, and technology, and appears confident that the American public will support and fund such a relationship.

Horace's Compromise

In contrast to the optimism in *Educating Americans for the 21st Century*, *Horace's Compromise* offers a sobering view of education. This report appreciates the characteristics of an ideal learning environment, but is not convinced these characteristics can be achieved in America's public schools any time in the near future. The reasons are complex, with the major issue being that the individual gets lost in the shadow of the institution. This is an individual-equity oriented document in which men and women are the measures of all schooling.

Horace's Compromise is about high school and adolescence. In adolescence, one must become serious about the future. Childhood is over. Fantasy succumbs to reality and students face major decisions about what they know, how they perform, where they are going, and under what conditions. Teachers' central task is to motivate and inspire these learners. But somehow in American schools the relationships have deteriorated. *Horace's Compromise* questions why.

The school described in *Horace's Compromise* is a dull bureaucracy. Teachers fail to realize that their primary reason for being is to enhance students' intellectual skills. According to this report, students should elect to go to secondary school because such choice is the first task of responsible citizenship and being active in the role of learner applies appropriately the skills mastered in school. Horace Smith makes mistakes, too. He treats his students as a standard group, failing to see their idiosyncratic beauty. He loses sight of the pleasure involved in struggling to learn something new, in rising above the circumstances of one situation and generating truths of a higher order, or giving power and autonomy as incentives for further effort. Horace cannot transcend his own personal situation, or escape his own failure to pass to his students a love of learning for its own sake, unrelated to the tawdry world around him. He misses the opportunity to be a hero even in the commonplace. In a sense, that is what *Horace's Compromise* expects of teachers, to help students realize that the greatest treasures reside in their own minds and abilities. This report is democratic equity writ large. It is a study that fights uniformity and seeks the active involvement of all the parties in the unique experience of learning.

In the last analysis, *Horace's Compromise* calls for a radical restructuring of secondary education. The intellectual skills it suggests provide the skeletal structure of subject matter; the integrated departments it proposes are the basis of a new school organization, but not the only possible design. The report leaves much to students and teachers to determine in their own collaborative way. After all, those who are responsible for education must adjust arrangements so that learning occurs in a personalized fashion. Obviously, recommendations on class size, teaching load, assessment, and staff preparation are derived from the essential relationship between the student and the teacher, unlike efficiency reports which focus on quantitative and not qualitative outcomes.

The high school this report envisions at the end of the century, in some ways, embodies *The Paideia Proposal's* axiom that the best education for the best is the best education for all. It is a public school established according to plans for a more select private institution. As *Horace's Compromise* depicts it, this new vision of schooling is far removed from the 'people's colleges' of the nineteenth century. No longer is the goal to build schools as havens of knowledge in a rough raw country facing a western frontier. In the new information age, America must enable all its citizens to use the abundant sources of information available everywhere. It is the people who count — more than the technology and more even than the state. *Horace's Compromise* questions how much the state can rightfully mandate for an individual's education. Public schooling has to leave room for human creativity, this reform report maintains it is the nation's creative genius currently at stake in educational reform.

The Emergent Problems of Reform

The analysis of reform reports shows that the dominant interest today is in the society-efficiency model of schooling. Reformers want schools that serve the needs and goals of society, and that have moral, political, and economic outcomes. The content-excellence model of schooling, although not quite as prominent, still commands significant attention, primarily because of its emphasis on subjects such as mathematics, science, and technology. Proponents of this model see the most important educational problems as the need for a cohesive curriculum and the need to increase instructional effectiveness. Finally, equity for the teacher as well as for the student forms the third major emphasis in the reports of the eighties. These documents are significant because they see the conditions of educational exchange formative not only for the individual but for the quality of life in the nation as well. Each model of schooling carries with it implications for policy and attitudes about human relations in the overall school system (see Figure 5).

How do the reforms of the eighties compare with those of other educational reform periods? Like most reform eras, the 1980s are exhibiting rapid social change and a need to clarify the purposes of education *for this time.* One might suggest, at first glance, that the eighties are similar to the times of Eliot's committee, the fight against

Figure 5. The Eight Reports and Their Goal Emphases

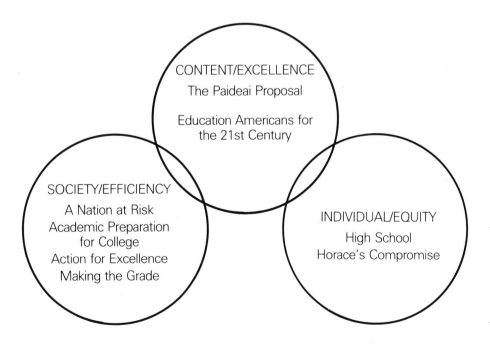

CONTENT/EXCELLENCE
The Paideai Proposal

Education Americans for
the 21st Century

SOCIETY/EFFICIENCY
A Nation at Risk
Academic Preparation
for College
Action for Excellence
Making the Grade

INDIVIDUAL/EQUITY
High School
Horace's Compromise

Progressivism, and the era of Sputnik and James Conant. Those reform periods concentrated on creating standards, especially for college entrance, and achieving consensus on the essential subjects, if not the competencies, of learning. But elements in the current reports reflect other reform periods, too. There is the need to respond to human experience, as advocated by *The Cardinal Principles*; apprehension about the diversity of the Amerian population and its tendency to become more heterogeneous, as after World War II; and a greater interest in how humans learn and create as reflective of the work of John Dewey and Jerome Bruner. Analyzing this current reform period is not merely ascribing 'either-or' classifications, but rather to see what problems emerge and how they are related to one another. A more holistic view of the current reform period rests on an appreciation of what the reports fail to consider as much as on what they actually discuss. What are the real problems that emerge from the reports of the eighties and what historical baggage inherited from other reform eras comes along with them?

The major problem facing America's schools is understanding intellectual pursuit and what it means for teachers and students to be engaged in an academic enterprise. Anti-intellectualism is an old evil in American educational history that still manifests itself in some of today's practices. As teachers come to respect their students, and school boards and administrators to trust their faculties, there will be formed the beginning of a community of scholars. Until then, however, there needs to be developed a new concept of human intelligence, not just for those who go to college, but also for those in the workplace, where the ability to think is no less important (National Academy of Sciences, 1984). Addressing this problem means forging a new mission for schools: teaching students how to think. All students need not only the basic skills, but also skills in higher order reasoning for living and working in a complex industrial world. The society-efficiency model of schooling deals with the standards associated with this mission. But standards, although significant, are not enough. Discovering how the content of the curriculum is related to thinking, especially in key disciplines such as mathematics, science, or computer technology, is another aspect of this problem. Equity concerns both of student and teacher dimensions are still another. *Balancing goal emphasis* is a major issue in sorting out the various reform reports. To pursue only one policy goal may bias an effort and leave other issues unattended, thereby jeopardizing the success of the reform process itself.

In combatting anti–intellectualism, one major fault of the reform process becomes apparent. The great chasm between elementary-secondary and higher education has to be bridged. The research capability of the many university disciplines that bear on education should be harnessed to help resolve some of the problems raised by the current reports. The period following the Committee of Ten's work and the early sixties after Bruner wrote *The Process of Education* are the only times that liberal arts professors joined educators to work collaboratively on the tasks of schooling. But collaboration among educators at all levels of schooling today assumes that no one group has a monopoly on understanding the intricacies of intellectual exchange. As *The Cardinal Principles* challenged the domination of colleges in setting educational standards, some of the current reports question whether higher education, the state, or business can dictate the basic criteria for sound schooling. As the teacher-proof curricula of the 1960s proved to be dysfunctional in the classroom, American education no longer can ignore the teachers' role in shaping programs and creating instructional materials. Lazerson, McLaughlin and McPherson (1984), warn university scholars not to make the mistakes of the 1960s in emphasizing subject content while neglecting the collaborative relationships with school staffs:

> They were enthusiastic about academic research and highly critical of school instruction. Their goal was to teach young students the structure of their discipline, to have them think like mathematicians, or social or natural scientists. They were less concerned about the realities of classroom teaching and more interested in intellectual discourse about the ideal instructional content. At best they were ambivalent toward school teachers. (p. 316)

The reform literature today provides a framework of goals around which the nation can carefully examine what it means to think and what kinds of efforts it takes to develop the skills of thinking in a diverse population.

This central academic concern then leads to two further problems elucidated by the reform reports: what is good pedagogy and how to address the multiple needs of youngsters in a population as hetero-geneous as that of the United States? The efficiency model of schooling suggests good teachers are those who enable their students to score high on achievement tests. In a highly competitive market, test scores are a serious consideration. But for developing a population that is keen at problem solving, they are much too narrow a focus for success. Good pedagogy involves knowing one's content and helping others to learn its intricacies; it means being able to inspire, but also to critique; it requires examining one's own practices and improving and changing those practices when necessary. The introduction of the computer in the classroom is a prime example of this kind of flexibility. Nearly all the current reform reports urge educators to quickly ensure that students are computer literate, whatever that term may mean. But a redefinition of pedagogy in the world headed for the twenty-first century cannot escape taking into account what computerization of society entails, how computers affect student learning, and how computerization is to be coordinated with the development of thinking in particular subject matters. Employing technology today is a bit like breaking with the classical curriculum in the days of the Committee of Ten. Moving into the world of modern languages and industrial science in 1893 was a daring, if not threatening, step.

Addressing student needs is obviously a necessary issue but not a comfortable one for several of the reform documents. Although every report calls for excellence and equity, few do as thorough a job of dealing with equity as they do with specifying excellence. Where equity concerns are discussed, the focus is largely on teachers: increase teachers' pay, lighten the teaching load, and improve professional status. The real question, it seems, should be how to enable all the youngsters in America to learn to use their minds. The problems of urban students and non-English speakers, in particular, need to be examined further. Few of the reports really face these complex issues. Many of the questions Conant raised in arguing for comprehensive secondary schools surface again and probably need to be readdressed in terms of a more contemporary mission for schooling. What role do parents and community play in enabling youngsters to take full advantage of schooling? How can discipline be balanced with student creativity and self-management? The critics point to the teacher's role in dealing with these problems. With the exception of *Horace's Compromise*, the reform reports ignore Bruner's immense contribution to understanding what the teacher's tasks actually entail. Such insensitivity on the part of the reform writers unfortunately shows the shallowness of present understanding about the nature of learning and the complexities of the instructional process.

Implementation issues, too, pose problems for reform. Who should lead the reform effort and who should pay for it? The reform reports indicate that collaboration and grass roots involvement are essential. In certain areas like data collection and research, a nationwide federal role seems necessary. Nonetheless, educators actually in schools are apt to remain the primary and most vital force in school improvement. Tasks must be determined, priorities set, and 'quick-fix' remedies discouraged. There is now an indication that some improvement efforts have been launched too hastily (Breckenridge, 1984), forcing school leaders to pull back on plans already set in motion. Let this be a lesson to reformers. Perhaps the historical perspective makes it easier to realize, as Larry Cuban (1983) expressed it,

> There is a profound difference between altering the conditions that shape what happens in schools (for example, introducing the longer school day and the California version of the New York Regents Test) and improving classroom teaching and student performance — a distinction authors of these efforts either fail to consider or judge unimportant. (p. 194)

The initial, and perhaps most critical task of any reform effort is to identify the problems that need to be resolved. The present reform period has amply accomplished this. The next task is to consider what resources can be applied to the emergent problems of reform.

Part III
Lessons for the Future

5   Changing America

Despite the similarities between reform movements, the context is never quite the same, the tools of reform are never quite the same, and neither the clients nor their problems are ever quite the same. Beneath the apparent circularity lie linear developments that have transformed both our social problems and our approaches to them.

Carl F. Kaestle, *Social Reform and the Urban School* (1978)

Lessons of Reform

Examining the eight reform reports from a historical perspective leads to several conclusions about the course of American public education. First is the extraordinary complexity of educational decision-making and policy development. Sound remedies rarely come in checklist form. The values of the Republic itself come into play in determining which reform recommendations are implemented and how. The reoccurrence of some of the same issues in successive reform periods may signal that a basic conflict is brewing between historical values and more current social, economic or political conditions.

The second lesson that emerges from a historical view is that educational reform is a long-range concern. The correction of past ills can rarely be accomplished both quickly and successfully at the same time. Reform efforts, suggests Howe (1983) usually involve many actors cooperating over a protracted period of time. The real value of the present reform period may be the opportunity it provides to look at existing conditions, understand the underlying conflicts and causes, and *plan for* long-range improvement. Tyler (1982) envisions effective and dynamic educational organizations as being able to 'anticipate and respond appropriately to changes in society' (p. 657); in a word, to lead reform rather than merely to react to crises.

Finally, the reform reports point up how much there is still to learn. Some issues, in fact, have hardly begun to be considered. It is not just that technical data are weak, as Stedman and Smith (1983) maintain, but that we have not formulated accurately the categories of information we need; nor do we know who should collect and analyze the data or how the results can be used in making sound decisions. There are lessons to be drawn from each of these conclusions and how well we learn them will ultimately shape the success with which reform is carried out in schools.

Changing American society constantly interacts with the lessons about reform that emerge from this study. That the United States finds itself a global entity is a circumstance unique to the current reform period. In 1957, after *Sputnik*, Americans bore the impact of worldwide industrial development. Educational reform at the time of Conant and Bruner was couched in terms of international competition and national security. Anxieties abated only when, several years later, the United States landed the first man on the moon. Today, however, that same anxiety has re-emerged, cloaked in economic and political fears, and hastened by a renaissance in technology and the threat of nuclear war. Perhaps for the first time, the nation is seriously looking at itself as a global competitor — and it does not necessarily like what it sees.

Demographic Changes

Several recent demographic studies (Bureau of the Census, 1984; Population changes will affect education policy, 1984; Urban schools: some statistics, 1984; Usdan, 1984) suggest that changes in America's population will profoundly effect education over the next few decades. A growing minority population, the aging of white America, and the changing role of women in the workplace are all generating new social conditions that will, one way or another, transform schools.

While nearly all of America's schools experienced population declines over the past decade, urban schools were hit with the double problem of adjusting to fewer students and 'white flight'. Today, minorities make up more than half the school enrollments in most of the nation's twenty-five largest cities. The Council of Great City Schools (Urban schools: some statistics, 1984) reports that increases in minority enrollments between 1970–1982 occurred largely in three categories: the percentage of blacks increased from 40.7 per cent to 47.2 per cent, Hispanic enrollment nearly doubled from 11.7 per cent to 21 per cent and the Asian student population increased from 1.4 per cent to 4.1 per cent. Age is another factor in characterizing student populations, for both now and the future. Black and Hispanic persons tend to become parents at a young age and generally have higher birth rates. Of the 16 million Hispanics now living in the United States. the fifth largest concentration of Spanish-speaking people in the western hemisphere, 20 per cent was, as of 1980, under 10 years old. This means that child bearing years are still ahead of most of the population. Combining these figures with the general aging pattern of the white population reinforces the contention in *Educating Americans for the 21st Century* that, by the turn of the century, many more of our schools will be serving a majority population made up of minority youngsters. What is happening in San Francisco is a case in point:

> San Francisco, which has always been an immigrant city, is rapidly becoming a third world city. According to the 1980 census, it is about 58 per cent white — compared with 89.5 per cent white in 1950 — and 12 per cent black. The big influx, much of it still uncounted is made up of Asians and Hispanics.
>
> Almost half the children in the San Franciso public school system come from homes where English is not the first language. The school district employs interpreters in twenty-six language groups. ('We lump some of the smaller languages together', says a district official.) The main groups are Spanish, Chinese, Filipino and Vietnamese, but the list of languages includes everything from Arabic to Punjabi, Samoan to Hmong. (Cohen, 1984, p. 4A)

The situation is not very different in New York, Los Angeles or Miami.

Traditionally, the largest Spanish-speaking communities in the United States have been in California and Texas, closely followed by Arizona, Colorado and New Mexico. But with prospects for employment luring more and more Hispanics into cities, communities in New York, Florida, Illinois, Michigan, Ohio, New Jersey and Pennsylvania are also beginning to feel the impact of this population shift (Mills, 1984).

The business world has long recognized the benefits of communicating with non-English speakers and, in at least two cities, Miami and Los Angeles, has issued yellow page telephone directories in Spanish.

That kind of readiness to accommodate recent arrivals has not always been shared by state governments. In order to avoid the cost and conflict of bilingual operations, Kentucky's legislature recently decreed that English is the state's official language (Kentucky rules, 1984). Nevertheless, the growth of non-English speaking populations in the United States is likely to make bilingualism or language deficiency a recurring theme in educational reform for a long time to come.

Changes in the Workplace

Changing labor patterns are another influence on school populations. Today, 51 per cent of American women are working outside the home; seven out of ten women aged 20 to 24 are now employed (Reagan, 1984). This rapid acceleration of women into the workforce has profound implications for the home from which the student comes. On the bright side of the picture is that families where both parents work, 62 per cent of US homes, generally have a higher average income (Sixty-two per cent of US families, 1984). But with more mothers absent from home, young children's lives are bound to be affected, although to what extent has yet to be fully examined. Other demographic developments have changed family life as well. Boyer (1984) points out that the number of families influenced by divorce has doubled since 1960. Nearly 20 per cent of America's homes are maintained by a single parent, most often by a woman who is either divorced, separated, widowed, or has never married. About half the students now entering elementary school will live in one-parent homes by the time they graduate from high school. Changes in the labor market have also affected the child's classroom: as new employment opportunities are opening up, women are leaving teaching for other careers. The years between 1970 and 1980 saw nearly 10 per cent fewer women on elementary faculties than in the decade before, and there is no reason to think that this downward trend will change in the foreseeable future.

While women are steadily strengthening their presence in the labor force, urban youth are faring considerably worse. Black and Hispanic teenagers represent only 19.7 per cent of the young people in the United States, but 29.4 per cent of unemployed youth (Reagan, 1984). The combination of low school achievement and lack of English language skills — speaking, reading, and writing — makes these groups the least likely to be absorbed by the labor market. Job competition from recent immigrants is compounding the problem further. Estimates on the percentage of undocumented workers in the US labor force range from 2 per cent to as high as 10 per cent (*Ibid*). Just as local communities are feeling the effects of these numbers in the classroom, urban youth are feeling their impact in the entry-level job market.

The US and the Global Village

Underlying many of the recommendations in the reform reports is America's view of itself as an international culture. Demographics speak to internal shifts in the country and are quantitative descriptions of change in American soceity. Some qualitative international dimensions are harder to capture. Glazer (The New Immigration, 1984) raises the issue of whether the recent waves of immigration from Asia and Latin America are not different from America's previous immigrant groups. He suggests that culturally the nation feels threatened by these newcomers and, so far, political groups have failed to reach consensus on how to respond. The question, says Glazer, is whether the nation will be overwhelmed by groups of poorly skilled immigrants, encroaching on already underskilled urban populations and poverty-ridden school systems? Carnoy (1983), in analyzing *The Paideia Proposal*, warns of the social conflict that may ensue if the matter is not speedily resolved. Others fear a shrinking middle class or a shift toward a more skewed and socially unacceptable distribution of income in the America of the future.

To some extent, America's industrial and technological race with Japan is part of this cultural threat. Americans are asking themselves whether the more authoritarian, submissive, and cooperative Japanese culture is better organized and trained to deliver the high technological products than their own country, and some are finding the answer disturbing (Lohr, 1984; Martin, 1984). Reform proposals should examine this view of cross-cultural competition in greater depth.

A view of America in the future, however, must go beyond current concerns and consider the job market that lies ahead. Technological advances present a whole new work agenda for large numbers of Americans but for others it signals job retrenchment or at least a shift from manual to mental abilities. Some researchers (Bluestone, 1985) foresee 'occupational skidding', as industrial workers lose jobs in basic industry and slip down the occupational hierarchy. Levin and Rumberger (1983) suggest that the fastest occupational growth will take place in service areas, and of these only two, teaching and nursing, will require post-secondary training. This means that future workers' ability to learn and be flexible in the workplace will be a major factor in future employability. Again, there is a challenge for the nation's schools.

How can lessons from the reform literature, and from academic research and practical knowledge, be applied to some of the dynamism evident in changing American society? Three major themes emerge from the current period of educational reform: understanding intellectual pursuit at the turn to the twenty-first century, meeting students' diverse needs, and determining good pedagogy. These are the problems to be addressed in evaluating the reform reports of the eighties.

6   *Thinking and Schooling*

Thinking is sometimes viewed as a complex skill or collection of skills. Given this view, it is natural to consider thinking to be something that may be done well or poorly, efficiently or inefficiently; and to assume that how to do it better is something one can learn.

Raymond S. Nickerson, David N. Perkins, and Edward E. Smith, *Teaching Thinking* (1984)

In Search of Skilled Thinking

If excellence in schooling is to be even partially equated with understanding intellectual pursuit, the mere setting of higher standards and adjusting to external conditions will not be enough to bring about reform. The efficiency-driven model of *A Nation at Risk*, *Academic Preparation for College*, *Action for Excellence*, and *Making the Grade* must somehow come to grips with the content and equity dimensions of the other reports. True reform has to attain superior education for *all* America's youth. The central problem in this challenge, according to one independent school head, is:

> How, exactly, does one transfer good teaching and educational resources efficiently into a learning process that stretches *each* student's mind and talents to the fullest and lays the foundation for a lifelong quest for knowledge? (Clement, 1983, p. 22)

In fairness, one should point out that *A Nation at Risk* recognizes this problem, but fails to address it fully:

> Excellence characterizes a *school* or *college* that sets high expectations and goals for all learners, *then tries in every way possible to help students reach them* [my emphasis added]. (p. 12)

91

The National Commission overlooked the fact that the responsibility of the school is to *know how to educate youngsters*, at least insofar as knowledge about teaching and learning is applicable to actual school situations. This may not necessarily reflect an anti-intellectual bias on the part of the Commission, but instead a myopic efficiency model that lacks a sense of history. In Clement's (1983) words, the National Commission 'embeds in its findings and recommendations a popular American myth: everything can be fixed; it takes only working harder to do so' (p. 20). The fact is that clarifying the purpose of education, as Bakalis (1983) proposes, or setting priorities for school reform, as Ravitch (1984) advises, requires identifying the qualitative and substantive aspects of teaching students how to become intelligent human beings. The current interest in thinking skills, problem solving, and reasoning in the school's program offers much food-for-thought in tackling this task (Beyer, 1983; Costa, 1981; Nickerson, 1982).

Thinking skills refer not only to what one learns, particular facts and information, but to the processes that integrate ideas into meaningful contexts. Competence in thinking creates individuals who are able to critique and reason, both salient features, suggests Giroux (1984), of citizens in a democratic society. Helping American students think better is a goal in all the reform reports, but only a few dig deeper into what it really means to think or what should be done to help students acquire higher order cognitive skills. It is fine to have 'high expectations', but unless students are given the means to fulfill these expectations, there cannot help but be disappointment in store. Fortunately, a number of research and development efforts, state and city activities, and university projects are engaged in this pursuit. Sternberg (Sternberg, 1981; Wagner and Sternberg, 1984) reported to the National Commission that there is growing acceptance of defining intelligence in terms of thinking and learning skills. Two other papers presented to the National Commission, by Doyle (1982) and Snow (1982), focus on the intricacies of teaching thinking including the sequence of skill development, the relationship of thinking to academic content, and specific teaching strategies to develop reasoning ability in youngsters. These matters are obviously central to enhancing student learning in the classroom; they are also basic to assessing achievement in any meaningful way. The issues are the same as those that underlie many of the reforms recommended in *Horace's Compromise* and *High School*, as well as in *Educating Americans for the 21st Century* and *The Paideia Proposal*. But they are rarely extensively explored in the reports.

The current movement for teaching thinking has some essential elements that are useful in understanding intellectual pursuit on a more practical level. Levin and Rumberger (1983), in looking at student skill development and future job application, see cognitive skills being more valuable than knowledge-particular subject matter. These researchers call for the development of many of the same skills designated by Secretary Bell (1983): evaluation and analysis, critical thinking, problem solving, organization and reference, synthesis, inference, and writing/composing. Educators are now working on defining these several kinds of thinking as well as explicating the underlying cognitive operations that constitute the individual skills (Beyer, 1984a and 1984b; Nickerson, Perkins and Smith, 1984). A summer 1984 conference at Harvard University, and a spring meeting at Wisconsin's Wingspread Foundation sponsored by the Association for Supervision and Curriculum Development, are but two examples of the extensive interest in this research area. Additionally, a number of instructional programs that specifically address thinking have been begun across the country.

Thinking and Metacognition

The movement for teaching thinking is highly reminiscent of Jerome Bruner's Woods Hole meeting nearly twenty-five years ago. Bruner (1960) stressed the importance of intuitive heuristics in learning and the student's involvement in the process of thinking. Today's thinking programs take the position that similar metacognitive skills can be taught and developed. In other words, suggests Beyer (1984), students can be directly taught to become aware of various thinking strategies, be conscious of the different ways to approach a problem and resolve it, and know when and how to use alternate higher order processes for greater achievement. Skills like 'process selection' or 'translation of feedback', suggests Sternberg (1981), have everyday application as well as academic significance. He points out that although these skills are inherent in developing intelligent behavior, standardized tests largely ignore them. Reform proposals to improve students' thinking abilities should not incur such a significant omission in either teaching or testing procedures.

Tied in with the metacognitive approach to thinking is the matter of equity. No longer is thinking just for college-bound students. Nor is it the exclusive domain of only the gifted and talented. Higher order processes and metacognitive skills are goals for all workers' job success in a technological economy. Cognitive researchers (Whimbey and Whimbey, 1975) maintain that all youngsters are capable of attaining such advanced processes, with the exception of the feebleminded. That only about half the population actually ever develops these skills, as Arlin (1975) maintains, may be a sign that secondary schools have failed in their responsibility in this area. It also suggests that a national effort in developing basic skills for all Americans must be accompanied by a similar continuous program in higher order processes if students are to use their basic education to the best advantage.

Curriculum and Instruction

Several tasks are subsumed in making thinking a primary goal of schooling. These have to do with the curriculum, its instruction, and its assessment. It is important to note here that although most of the reports concentrate on reform in the high school (*The Paideia Proposal* and *Educating Americans for the 21st Century* are the exceptions) the development of thinking skills has a place throughout the elementary and secondary program. Passow (1984) remarks that one can hardly take on more advanced study in science and mathematics without the prerequisite skills. In this respect, many of the developmental issues raised by Piaget and Bruner in earlier reform periods are still relevant today. Yet, while several current reports recognize the significance of early intervention, they leave others to answer the question, 'early intervention of what?'. Some of the new thinking skills programs may suggest answers to this question. They may also help explain the relationships between basic and more advanced cognitive processes in the overall school curriculum.

Including thinking and reasoning in the school program does not imply that there should be one course of study for all students, as advocated in *The Paideia Proposal*. Instead, the concept is more in line with reports which urge a 'core of common studies' (Resnick and Resnick, 1983) or a program of 'general education' (Tanner, 1984; Offermann, 1984). Finn (1984) suggests there are two obvious ways for schools to include thinking skills in their curricula. One is to make them part of the school's core program; the second is to incorporate them into the sequence of knowledge development specified by state or district standards. The development of thinking might best contribute to such a common core by serving as a central organizer for a variety of curricula. Using this approach, Eisner (1983) calls for balance in school programs and stresses the importance of multiple forms of learning. Similarly, Broudy's (1982) ingredients in a K–12 curriculum resemble those in *Horace's Compromise*, but are less historically oriented. The current wisdom seems to be not to focus on standardized specific content in such courses, but to stress process and alter course content as needs change. This kind of flexibility has the extra benefit of avoiding some of the coverage problems raised in *Horace's Compromise* and, equally important, encourages educators to explore the possibilities of integrated learning across several disciplines.

There is a dramatic difference between a thinking-oriented approach to curriculum development and the 'new' subjects developed after Bruner wrote *The Process of Education* in 1960. That reform period was discipline or subject-centered and focused, by and large, on students becoming expert researchers and 'discovering' learning for themselves. Package developers tried to create materials directly for the classroom, by-passing teachers and, to some extent, forgetting the development of the learners as well. Sixth graders are sixth graders, not junior scientists. To develop thinkers today does not require imitating scientists, as the strict content-excellence approach would suggest. Rather, sound thinking programs need to capture the *spirit* of scientific inquiry and encourage teachers to help students develop the fluency of skills that enables them to become independent researchers. Broudy (1982) calls this the power of interpretive thinking, the finest example of the reasoning critic. This position parallels the current emphasis on metacognitive qualities. Consider a case in point: Stein (1983) discovered that many teenagers are astonishingly ignorant of recent history. What is tragic about their ignorance is not only that they do not know the facts, but that they also do not know *how* to remedy their condition. The focus on reasoning and thinking today seeks intellectual autonomy as a major goal of schooling and expects that eventually students can and will pursue independently the knowledge they need. Kamii (1984) maintains such individual autonomy is a major aspect of Piaget's theory. Eisner (1983) argues that it is a mainstay of all sound instruction. Both views are consistent with equity-driven goals of schooling.

Curriculum for thinking skills must also be open to different kinds of knowledge and ways of learning. When *A Nation at Risk* and *Academic Preparation for College* cite SAT scores as measures of achievement, they are focusing only on verbal and numerical ability. These are the primary objectives of most basic education programs, but they are not the only possible ones. Gardner's (1983) recent study of the human mind identifies seven separate intelligences — linguistic, musical, logical-mathematical, spatial, bodily-kinesthetic, interpersonal, and intra-personal — that can be developed in all students. It may be that the progression of each intelligence influences the individual's overall ability development. If so, curricula must be prepared, in some degree, to respond to all of these kinds of knowledge, not just to what is ordinarily thought of as 'the basic skills'. It is also possible that how information is presented to learners influences their development of reasoning skills. In order to give students the greatest opportunity to learn these skills, Beyer (1984b) suggests that pupils practice them in contexts other than the way they were introduced. Eisner (1982) calls for including different forms of learning, particularly the expressive and mimetic modes, in every child's education. Issues such as these are central to determining curriculum for sophisticated cognitive processes. Had the writers of the reform reports considered them, their positions on academic development may have been quite different.

Like *The Cardinal Principles of Secondary Education* before it, Boyer's *High School* maintains that mastery of English is key to being an educated person in our society. Even Eliot's Committee designed four curricular programs around models of linguistic knowledge: Classical, Latin-Scientific, Modern, and English (see Appendix A). Boyer, though, goes further and relates language, both writing and speaking, to thought. He is not incorrect in his advocacy, but his emphasis is probably skewed insofar as developing a comprehensive and coherent curriculum. Language is not the only symbol system available to humans. Clear thinking may develop from several modes — numerical and spatial — as well as linguistic. Boyer hopes for a new, interdisciplinary vision in the classroom, but it is unlikely that his Core of Common Learning, based as it is mainly on language, will provide that. Eight-and-a-half of the units he ascribes to the high school program (out to fourteen-and-a-half) are language-oriented. Boyer notes the challenge of technology to our current school program, but he does little exploration of what processes or learnings underlie technology, science, or mathematics. Recent research in these areas suggests there are spatial aspects of multiple dimensionality that need to be addressed in instruction (Senechal and Fleck, 1985). The work of Feuerstein and his associates (1981) on cognitive modifiability in teenagers maintains that poorly performing students are deficient in more than linguistic ability. The comparison of American education to the Japanese system raises other interesting questions relative to visual and gestalt input. With no arts in the program, Eisner (1983) for one would find the richness of the Boyer curriculum quite suspect.

Perhaps *High School* needs to broaden its view of 'the core of common learning'.

The Challenge of Computers

The integration of computers into school programs is probably the most significant issue in the study of symbol development by other than linguistic means today. With the exception of *Horace's Compromise*, all the reform reports call for development of computer literacy in relatively urgent terms. What is meant by computer literacy though, beyond the need to be familiar and operative with machinery, is not extensively discussed in most reports. The observation skills mentioned in *Academic Preparation for College* may be an area worthy of study with regard to computers and thinking ability, but this track is not pursued either. Bruner (1966) acknowleges that the progression from enactive representation to iconic and then to symbolic formations is simply not well understood. Olsen (1973 and 1976) suggests the relationships of culture, technology, and intellect are key to developing the school's programs.

After twenty years of experience with television and computers, what do we really know about visual and manipulative input to thinking and learning? Most of the reform reports acknowledge that a whole new technology is upon us, and obviously the sciences and mathematics are highly influenced by its development, but what direction does this technology give to the overall education of young students? Education still must develop a way to integrate computers and cognitive science research into school experiences so that their use is consistent with the full development of higher order skills. Sloan (1984) reminds us that 'concrete-operation skills of technical reason' or 'functional, utilitarian language' are not sufficient. Humans are capable of much more. He argues for a higher level, qualitative knowing that seeks to bridge both rationality and emotions. Dreyfus and Dreyfus (1984) warn of the potential danger that computers can pose in hindering the development of intuitive proficiency and expertise, two characteristics of creative learners. The work of Brown (1983 and 1984) suggests, however, that computers can become 'exceptional learning environments' to enhance student thought processes. Resolving these differing positions and extending research on computers and cognition, similar to the studies begun by Klein (1985), are tasks it seems we cannot afford to ignore, if we are to achieve the democratic vision of the learner that has been a persistent theme of American educational reform.

Thinking and Testing

Finally, understanding intellectual pursuit demands an examination of how students are assessed. Testing and test data play an important role in most of the reform reports, but reference in those documents is made almost wholly to standardized achievement testing. Other types of evaluation may be just as valuable, as, for instance, the National Assessment for Educational Progress' examination of general characteristics of American youngsters (Mullis, 1984), cross-cultural comparisons completed by Husén (1983) and Stevenson (Irwin, 1984), and the Evaluation of Educational Achievement (Bridgman, 1984).

Another important question to raise about thinking and testing is what kinds of testing are appropriate to assess learners' thought processes. Normed achievement tests are primarily efficiency-driven instruments. They attempt to measure relatively discrete operations and are somewhat removed from the complexities of specific subject matter (Resnick and Resnick, 1983). As mentioned earlier, these achievement batteries are primarily power tests in verbal and quantitative skills. Sternberg (1981) notes that only one section of the Stanford Achievement Test attempts to examine arithmetic problem-solving ability as something apart from the actual completion of the problems. And Beyer (1984) indicates that even most professionally-developed critical thinking instruments fail to share with teachers descriptions or models of the skills that are the basis for the test items. The point is that commonly used achievement or ability tests are intended as sorting devices, not instructional tools. Criterion-referenced materials, which play a limited role in the reform reports, place greater emphasis on matching the content of instruction to the evaluation instrument and so have a greater potential of achieving 'excellence'. In addition, their outcomes are frequently better indicators of school accountability in meeting local goals than are more standardized test scores. Parties interested in raising student achievement in specific subject areas, as are the authors of *Making the Grade* and *Educating Americans for the 21st Century*, might particularly be better off determining progress with criterion rather than norm-referenced instruments. Not only the content but also the thinking processes within subject matters can be better evaluated by these tests.

There are, of course, those persons who question whether anything having to do with individual student progress can be 'measured'. Kirst (South-eastern states consider comparative testing, 1984) suggests that comprehensive measurement involves much more than testing, and should include other assessments such as time spent on homework and number and type of assignments completed. Cuban (1983 and 1984) maintains that linking testing policy to improvement efforts in curriculum and instruction, and especially to long-range plans for program and staff development, offers still another route to progress. He also argues that thinking skills must be a part of every teacher's repertoire, and receive just as much emphasis in the testing program as other skills.

Testing today, like curricula, must respond to different kinds of knowledge and learning. One test at one time is not a very complete measure of anything according to the individually-driven model of schooling. According to *Horace's Compromise*, 'mastery' of an individual student's work should be judged by an instructor who can create his or her mechanisms for assessing what the student knows. Sizer would probably agree with the following analysis in showing how far off course efficiency measures are in revealing anything truly significant about the abilities of America's youth:

> Using standardized tests as the sole measure of educational excellence, however, confuses the medium and the message. The measure is ill-suited to the goal. Standardized, multiple-choice achievement tests do not, of course, measure creativity. They assess one's ability to find what someone else has already decided is the one best answer to a pre-determined question. The tests do not measure the most important aspects of problem-solving ability — the ability to consider and evaluate alternatives, to speculate on the meaning of an idea based on first-hand knowledge of the world, to synthesize and interpret diverse kinds of information, to develop original solutions to problems.
>
> Moreover, the tests do not really measure performance of any kind. Performance, of course, means the ability to do something; it is active and creative. Recognizing a correct answer out of a predetermined list of responses is fundamentally different from the act of reading, or writing, or speaking, or reasoning, or dancing, or anything else that human beings do in the real world. (Darling-Hammond, 1984b)

In light of the importance that all the reform reports attribute to higher order cognitive skills, it would be folly for educators not to take into account how student performance in these skills is assessed, as well as how students are taught for such performance.

Children, like adults, protect themselves if they can from revealing their feelings when they are too painful or in situations where to do so may be risky. As teachers, our goal is to *understand* children, not to disturb them. To attempt to force a child's reaction may negate the very thing we are hoping to achieve.

Millie Almy, *Ways of Studying Children* (1975)

Missing: A Public Education for All Students

If thinking and other skills are to be within reach of all students, America must shed itself of racial, linguistic, and class biases in its educational system. The job of schools is to educate and socialize, not to be sorting grounds for haves and have-nots or knows and know-nots. Usdan's (1984) demographic data on America of the 1990s show that our educational system has a 'transcendent stake' in improving educational opportunities for all youngsters in our population. But, meeting student needs is probably the most amorphous and difficult task to face in reforming American education.

Students needs are as diverse as the pupils in our school population. Education's role can be made more manageable, however, by identifying the population groups that pose the most serious challenges for the decades ahead. In a way, the reform reports did that — mainly by considering the needs of more able students. Recommendations for improving performance in mathematics, science, and computer literacy are generally directed to the needs of gifted and talented youngsters or to higher-achieving groups. Concern of SAT or ACT scores focuses on the college-bound. By and large, the reform reports of the eighties neglect the educational welfare of youngsters in the urban underclass of American society.

High School touches on the curricular problems of teaching minority children and *Making the Grade* discusses bilingualism, but a substantive analysis of urban or minority educational needs is not pursued in any of the eight reports. Several writers note this omission as one of the weakest aspects of the current reform literature (Howe, 1983; Passow, 1984). Trying to explain this situation away by claiming that the overall goal of the reports is to improve education *for society's sake* is naive. Americans do not live in a homogeneous society. It is just as untenable to suggest that the distinguished panel members were unaware of actual conditions in urban schools. If the reform reports really seek to improve education for the nation's competitive advantage, there is no greater group of students 'at risk' than the youngsters of poor and minority families.

The Needs of Minority Youth

One of the first lessons about youth in the inner city is that they are not a cultural monolith. Black, Hispanic, or Asian — each group has its own experiences that do not fit into the national norm and its own way of interpreting those experiences. In the ghettos and barrios of big cities, family, work, education, and spirituality are often approached differently than in the suburbs and small towns of America. The minority child is developmentally influenced by his or her dominant experience, less so by an essentially alien mainstream culture. This poses a potentially grave conflict for schooling, especially if students are not highly motivated to learn or if the youngsters' sub-culture presents its own obstacles to achievement in the larger society. That is essentially the urban dilemma skirted by most of the current reform reports — to raise standards and demand better performance could only exacerbate what is already a precarious situation.

Glazer (1984) says about achievement and race, 'All the reports make a bow in the direction of minority needs; none of them face up to the reality that raising minimum standards and imposing minimum requirements simply increase the failure rate among Blacks' (p. 311). Loeb (1984a) suggests that combatting failure by requiring academic courses or mandating passing test scores is apt only to increase dropout rates among black youngsters from the inner city. The national average dropout rate has already climbed from 22.8 per cent in 1972 to 27.2

per cent in 1982 (Report Card, 1984). It would certainly seem, even to a relatively unastute observer, that the nation cannot afford the present school dropout rate, never mind a higher one.

Another issue influencing student needs is the increase in the number of children living in poverty. The negative relationship between poverty and school performance is one of the constants established by the National Assessment of Educational Progress: 'As in virtually all areas assessed by the National Assessment, disadvantaged-urban students perform below national averages, while advantaged-urban students perform above national averages' (Analyzing Literature 'difficult' for Many, 1981, p. 1). Higher numbers of poor youngsters, suggest some children's advocates, increase chances of a permanent underclass in America.

Compounding the poverty associated with life in the inner city are highly negative social influences on the black family including divorce, unemployment, drug abuse, and teenage pregnancy rates much higher than in the rest of the population (Haskins, 1983; Marquez, 1984). A recent study at the University of Michigan points out that low-income working mothers are most effected by these pressures. It also cites recent reductions in Aid to Families with Dependent Children as particularly harmful to black urban youth (AFDC Cuts Hurt, 1984).

It is important to realize that recommendations made by the reform commissions inevitably interact with already existing practices. Consider the problem of special education. There is growing awareness that the number of black students in classes for the learning disabled or emotionally impaired is inordinately high (McCormick, 1984). One can probably say that the reverse is true in programs for the gifted and talented. Even before the current reform period, educators widely recognized the need to identify treatments and strategies which might improve the skills of urban black youngsters. But for what goals? Questions should have been raised about the content-excellence and equity dimensions as well as about efficiency. What learnings had been missing in these students' previous educational programs? What skills do they fail to manifest and how can teachers develop them? Given the problematic factors in black youngsters' social and familial environ-ments, what remedial instruction can best compensate for academic deficiencies? Because answers to these problems are not forthcoming, say some researchers, black urban students' performance remains poor (Slobodzian, 1984) and the convenient but devastating practice of social promotion becomes entrenched in our educational system (Loeb, 1984b). If these same questions continue to go unanswered, the imposition of new standards and more exact testing requirements may actually build a new form of racial segregation in American society.

Focus on Hispanic Students

In some ways, challenges posed by Hispanic students are the same as those presented by America's black population. In other ways, there are unique cultural factors associated with the education of Latino youngsters. First, all Hispanic groups are not singularly oriented: Puerto Ricans differ from Mexicans; similarly, Cubans, Argentinians, and Salvadorans all came to the United States with different cultural histories and traditions. Moreover, Hispanic immigrants are not necessarily like other immigrant groups who enter this country. Most Hispanics arrive with big families and tend to settle in the barrios of large cities where life is often outside the urban mainstream of city politics. Their dreams of prosperity quickly fade in the face of urban poverty. Unlike Korean or Vietnamese immigrants, Hispanics are not particularly motivated to join the dominant culture or to have their children succeed rapidly in the world of business and technology. In the segregated areas of New York, Miami, Philadelphia, and Newark, a Hispanic immigrant can, fairly easily, go about life speaking only Spanish, or very limitedly, English. Many of these immigrants are undocumented and may even intend to return to their original homeland at a later date — a reason why some resist learning English or even using it. A recent survey reveals that at least 50 per cent of Hispanic Americans think of themselves as Hispanics first and Americans second, and more than eight out of ten say that the Spanish language is central to maintaining and fostering their cultural identity (Yankelovich, Skelly and White, 1984). Spanish-language telephone directories and cable television stations have lately bolstered this cultural perspective. Hispanics are also learning the value of operating as a united political block. But what is happening to the Hispanic child in school?

Language deficiency in English is the most obvious problem in educating Hispanic children, but this is only a part of a larger and more complex picture. The troubling fact is that many Spanish-speaking students are not functioning at higher cognitive operations in either language, and as a result, the dropout rate among Hispanic youngsters is inordinately high. In Chicago, for instance, it is reported at a staggering 70 per cent (Shipp, 1984). The national dropout rate among Hispanics is estimated to be more than double that of the general population (Ford to Nearly Double Program Support for Hispanics, 1984).

Only two of the current reform reports address the problems of Hispanic education in American schools and, interestingly, they approach the subject in very different ways. Basing its recommendation on the size of the immigrant group, its anticipated growth, and America's increased relations with other western hemisphere nations, *High School* suggests that Spanish be taught as a second language in all American schools. In contrast, *Making the Grade* recommends that the federal government insist upon the development of literacy in English as the first priority in elementary and secondary schooling. To help finance this effort, the latter report proposes using current bilingual education funds to teach English to non-English speakers.

From the society-efficiency point of view, there is no doubt that proficiency in the English language is a desirable characteristic for all Americans. As English is the *lingua franca* of the world of business, it should be the currency of instructional exchange in the classroom. It is certainly more convenient and cheaper for the state to operate in only one language. Still, it remains to be seen whether laws such as the one recently enacted in Kentucky are declared constitutional. From the content-excellence perspective, one could argue that most of the literary heritage of American society is in English, and that operating in the majority culture and understanding its history requires mastery of English. The trouble arises when these perspectives are thrown into conflict with real life experiences of non-English speaking individuals.

Hearing and speaking are important aspects of the Hispanic child's life. His or hers is a very verbal existence — sound, music, and conversation are all at a much faster tempo than their English equivalents. In school, the Hispanic youngster must learn to read, write, and play in English. Initially, at least, this is an alien experience that clashes with the child's perception of normal 'American' life. From the teacher's perspective, teaching youngsters with differing English language ability, along with the other usual variations of youthful behavior, makes instructing a class of thirty or thirty-five urban children all the more difficult.

These two perspectives — the child's and the teacher's — reveal a complex array of factors involved in the instruction of language-deficient children. One can set standards and goals and seek to reach them as an expression of well-meaning intent, but the process of actually accomplishing the outcome or product must be keyed to the constraints and possibilities of the persons who are the subjects of such activity. In that respect, educational policy-makers may need a better understanding of the dilemmas facing Hispanic students and their teachers in American schools.

The reform recommendations in *Making the Grade* are an interesting base from which to begin discussion of the Hispanic child's needs. When the report's authors recommended transferring bilingual funds to programs that teach English to non-English speaking children, Carlos R. Hortas, Chairman of the Department of Romance Languages at Hunter College, dissented. Hortas concurred that young Americans need to know how to function in English, but disputed the contention that abandoning bilingual instruction for the exclusive use of English would create a 'healthy learning environment' (*Making the Grade*, 1983, p. 12). Instead, he suggested that another proposal, using federal impact aid to help school districts experiencing particularly high rates of immigration, be extended to local financing of language instruction. Hortas further advocated second language training for all teachers, a recommendation supported by Brewster Denny and Patricia Albjerg Graham.

At least three separate arguments appear to be at issue in *Making the Grade*. First, there seems to be confusion surrounding the meaning and intent of bilingual instruction. At one point, the report summarizes its position:

> The best way to ensure the nation's linguistic resources is to make literacy in English the primary objective and to promote literacy in a second language as a valuable supplement to, not a substitute for, English. (p. 14)

Hortas rebutts:

> No bilingual program in the United States promotes another language as a *substitute for English*. In fact, intensive English instruction is a part of every bilingual program. Bilingual programs attempt to show that English is not, in and of itself, a superior or richer language than the student's native language. There is a greater social benefit in promoting and encouraging linguistic diversity than in calling for specious uniformity. (p. 14)

Hortas is addressing multicultural aspects of language instruction, as well as motivation factors in the classroom. What better way to welcome youngsters into the larger culture than to use their own language in teaching them the values of diversity in a democratic

Republic? The report's authors, with the exception of Hortas, also disregard the benefits of offering both languages to all students. In discussing the reports of the eighties, Boyer (1984) raises these very points:

> Offering all students an opportunity to study English *and* Spanish is one valuable way to demonstrate cultural diversity and to encourage the understanding necessary for national unity, as well. I am certain that the success of our schools, as well as the integrity of the nation, will depend on our capacity to achieve unity with diversity in America. (p. 529)

Bilingual instruction is as much a cultural exchange as a linguistic one. One learns to speak a language not merely to reproduce words but to share information and generate common meanings. Irving (1984) points out that communication, not just speaking, is the primary goal of a bilingual classroom. In so far as motivation and positive social experience stem from communication, bilingual education offers not a threat to national unity, as so many of the authors of *Making the Grade* fear, but one of the brightest prospects for its achievement.

A second issue raised in *Making the Grade* is the extent and cost of appropriate language instruction for language-deficient students. Whatever the appropriate program design, there is consensus that the earlier the intervention the better. The need for more sound foreign language instruction programs in elementary schools is so pervasive that it is one of the few areas in which all the reform reports generally concur. *A Nation at Risk* recommends that foreign language instruction for all students be started in elementary grades to serve 'the Nation's needs in commerce, diplomacy, defense, and education' (p. 26). But little is said about how to finance this endeavor, or where to find the personnel able to implement it.

The dilemmas introduced by foreign language instruction are a microcosm of the difficulties of reform efforts in general. Reformers like to set standards but fail to come to grips with the real hard issues at hand, such as where the money is to come from to support reform. Improverished urban school districts have enough difficulty meeting their usual personnel, curricular, and financial demands, let alone start-up costs of new programs. This difficulty characterizes the problem that reform efforts, both past and present, have in really dealing with critical issues of edcuation, especially in our urban areas. As one scholar observed, the reports often mask genuine problems by dealing with unexamined premises:

The implicit assumption in many of these reports is that disadvantaged youngsters are really no different from other students and to believe otherwise is both anti-intellectual and anti-democratic. (Passow, 1984, p. 680)

Finally, the topic of foreign language instruction opens an old wound in educational reform. It shows us that America's goals have never been well-met in this area. *Making the Grade* recommends that foreign language study be available to every student in American schools. Other reports, such as *High School*, call for foreign language studies as part of the high school curriculum or as a requisite of the secondary diploma. A quarter of a century ago, James Conant (1959) called for four years instruction in one foreign language for every American student in the comprehensive high school. His goal was mastery of that language, including the ability to read its literature and to converse fluently 'with an inhabitant of the country in question' (p. 69). But perhaps here is a point where the reform documents challenge current realities. Roslyn Yalow, a Nobel Prize-winning scientist, dissents from the recommendations in *Making the Grade*:

I really doubt the desirability of recommending that all high school students be required to study a foreign language. Is such competency really necessary for a farmer in Iowa, a coal miner in West Virginia, or a factory worker in the textile mills of the south? It might be highly desirable for a shopkeeper or a secretary in a bilingual community. The extent of competency, whether it should be ability to read, write, or speak fluently, should depend on personal and professional interests. (p. 13)

Yalow's reasoning is oriented to the efficiency model. The potential of the youngster is not at question; nor is the intellectual inspiration that mastery of a content area may offer under consideration.

Inherent Problems of Reform

Reform standards lay bare the values of a society. They force the nitty-gritty of our lives to stand alongside our values, and our values to be tested against given knowledge at any particular time. With regard to foreign language study, some important educational questions still need to be raised as American schools consider reform. For instance, years ago, Wilder Penfield, the neurosurgeon, suggested that bilingual experience actually enhances all linguistic capability, a thesis that was supported by his later research (Penfield, 1964 and 1975). How does that knowledge affect our current educational goals? Information about the extent to which learning a second or foreign tongue influences the rate of learning also warrants examination. Peterson (1983) suggests that *Making the Grade* neglected to ask the essential question:

> Does a child learn English more quickly if taught only in the English language? Or does the child master English more quickly and acquire greater self-confidence if, while learning English, he or she is taught other subject matters in his or her native tongue? (p. 7)

Recent research comparing monolingual children with bilingual youngsters in terms of cognitive skill development suggests positive answers to these questions (Durán, 1983).

And the very issue of why learn a foreign language at all still seems unclear in America's national perspective. It is possible that teaching English as a second language may be the key to helping youngsters master their deficiency. Perhaps in a generation or two the current Hispanic problem will go away. Perhaps it won't. Parochial America may choose to stay linguistically isolated from non-English speaking peoples. Then again, there always seems to be the problem of paucity of language teachers. These multi-faceted problems crop up over and over again when reform groups demand more rigorous education in American schools. At least in addressing current situations in the urban centers of our country, a new perspective may finally be emerging on bilingualism. Unlike Conant's time, today Americans need second language skills in order to be able to communicate with *fellow* Americans. That preparation ought to begin in early childhood. For students, as well as teachers, waiting for personal choice to manifest itself in foreign language study may be too late for a global society. Some say it is already too late for the world of international business.

Two countering forces seem to influence the needs of urban youngsters in this period of school reform. The first is the ability of urban districts to conform to the new standards by establishing appropriate educational programs. The second is the ability to offer these programs in ways that suit individual students in an urban environment. Goodlad (1983) has charactertized these forces as 'demo-cratization of knowledge' and the 'humanization of knowledge'. On both counts, urban schools seem to be in difficulty. Dropout rates are admissions of failed opportunity; to develop higher level mental processes one needs to stay in school. Howe (1984) suggests we had better measure schools' 'holding power' if we want the gains made by minority students to continue, and he urges that a new section of Title I be established to help keep urban youngsters in high school.

Humanization, in particular, brings up the subject of motivation and personalized instruction. Many urban students are unaware of the importance of higher order cognitive skills for future work or study. Farrer, Neufeld and Miles (1984) note the significance of the survey reported in Goodlad's *Study of Schooling* which indicates that more than 50 per cent of the teachers, parents, and students interviewed 'did not see intellectual development as the desired primary function of schooling' (p. 703). How much more is this the case in city schools? The teacher's ability to mediate instruction is the key to intellectually challenging urban adolescents. To break through the language barrier, to see education as more than just something leading to employment, to overcome the failings of home and family, and to build multiple skills for later development are part of that mediation. Feuerstein (1980), the Israeli psychologist, suggests that education of all children, but particularly disadvantaged youngsters, demands mediated learning and many American researchers agree (Cordes, 1984). Costa (1984), a leader in the thinking skills movement, maintains that 'mediating the metacognitive' is the essence of schooling at the end of the twentieth century.

The reform reports propose some practices in urban settings that ought to be studied further. Creating alternate educational experiences, changing tracking or ability grouping, developing motivation and self-discipline programs, and examining junior high or middle school readiness all merit examination. Nonetheless, realistic recommendations on enhancing and enriching the education of urban students deserve special attention, and these are sorely missing in the current reform reports.

8   *The Profession of Teaching*

There is a proverb about the difficulty of seeing the wood because of the trees. That difficulty is exactly the point which I am enforcing. The problem of education is to make the pupil see the wood by means of the trees.

Alfred North Whitehead, *The Aims of Education* (1929)

Good Teachers are Professional

No discussion of schooling and society can escape the question, Who is a good teacher? and its corollary, What is the profession of teaching? In the last analysis, all critiques of schooling rest on whether the teaching has been, is capable of, or ever will be effective.

In advocating one or another view of education, each of the reform reports — either consciously or not — adheres to a particular vision of good schooling. It follows, then, that various roles teachers play in school, and even outside it, influence a report's assessment of the educational scene.

The teacher's role in the educational process has a dual orientation: one is primarily student-focused and deals with pedagogy; the second extends to relationships the teacher has with other persons who influence the child's education in the school building, in the district, and even in the home or neighborhood. According to their conception of teaching, the reform reports vary in their discussions of these two orientations.

There is little disagreement in the reform documents on the need for teachers to be masters of some particular subject matter. Although different reports show a preference for one content over another — *High School's* emphasis on language; *Educating Americans for the 21st Century's* interest in science and mathematics; *The Paideia Proposal's* partiality for the humanities — they all associate good teaching with knowing some particular area in depth. Where their approaches diverge is in how to use that knowledge in the classroom. *A Nation at Risk* talks about nurturing students and imparting subject matter, but hardly mentions what pedagogy emanates from these actions. *Academic Preparation for College* discusses the importance of teachers imparting skills to students in various competency areas but does not really say how. The same void appears in *Action for Excellence*. In short, advocates of efficiency-oriented schooling generally direct their reforms to external conditions affecting the hiring and retaining of personnel, not to the pedagogical processes themselves.

The Paideia Proposal, Making the Grade, and *High School* acknowledge that teaching involves more than 'pouring in content' and that instructional improvement requires more than setting up a summer institute to upgrade teachers' subject matter mastery. Beyond that, however, all three reports go about examining effective teaching differently. *The Paideia Proposal* delineates at least three kinds of teaching — didactic, coaching-supervising, and Socratic questioning — and poses the question of how to coordinate these modes with instructional materials and student needs. *Making the Grade* delves into the inner workings of the learning process and calls for more research into the best methods of teaching mathematics and science, as well as more emphasis on remediation. *High School* not only challenges teachers to expect more from their students, but also, to do it more consistently. It also encourages them to heed new technology and to seek interdisciplinary meaning in the concepts they teach.

The remaining reports go into considerable depth in spelling out the tasks of teaching. *Educating Americans for the 21st Century* and *Horace's Compromise* examine how to improve student's cognitive performance, what teachers can do to inspire and involve students in classroom activities, and how to link school learning to out-of-school experiences. In spite of their detail, however, these reports, too, fall short of providing a master formula for good teaching. *Horace's Compromise* concludes that the craft of teaching remains largely 'intuitive, serendipitous, and even mysterious'. (p. 191)

With such an array of perspectives on teaching, and with each posing its own set of problems, what research findings can be brought to bear on pedagogy in educational reform? Several themes appear over and over again in the literature on improving staff capability. First, there is the quality of interaction in the classroom. Snow (1982), in his paper for the National Commission, calls upon teachers to be adaptive in their instructional methods in order to allow for a variety of learning experiences:

> Instruction must be geared to meet students where they are cognitively and motivationally; it must be adapted to capitalize on students' present strengths and to compensate for present weaknesses, even while attempting to remove those weaknesses for the future. It is possible to train directly the cognitive and metacognitive processing skills involved in intelligent learning and it is possible to prompt intrinsically motivated learning by intelligent arrangement of educational conditions. (p. 10)

Similarly, Feuerstein (1980) maintains that the teacher's most important role is to be a mediator of learning, someone who *enables* the child to learn. The focus of his approach is to change the child's cognitive organization through the activity of learning. Such mediation is the heart of classroom exchange.

Instilling in children the responsibility to learn autonomously is, then, another consideration in improving instruction. To improve teachers' classroom strategies, the literature suggests several types of practices. Some of these have to do with a teacher's ability to question students during instruction and to compose challenging test items, remembering that the task is not to trick or stymie but to expand the mind. Other practices focus on formulating assignments, using materials and textbooks, or relating teaching to curriculum. Still another fruitful approach, especially in the teaching of specific subject matter, is to identify why students are making particular errors, determine why certain misconceptions arose, and then correct them through alternate instruction.

The point is that every teacher manages a classroom environment. In this respect, monitoring student progress becomes just as important as introducing specific content materials. Similarly, classroom management involves paying attention to the quality of human exchanges. How students interact with the teacher and among themselves, and how both the teacher and the students conceive of schooling and learning can either encourage learning or discourage it. Phrases like 'cooperative interdependence among students' (Johnson, Johnson, Holubec and Roy, 1984); 'reciprocal teaching' (Palincsas and Brown, 1984); 'tutoring within group instruction' (Bloom, 1984); 'cooperative learning' (Slavin, 1983); and 'participation structures' (Doyle, 1982) illustrate that classroom instruction need not be a lonely endeavor.

The Collaborative Art of Teaching

The notion of school as a community dates at least as far back as the philosophy of John Dewey, but more recent observers of school life have begun to look at the school as a socio-cultural institution. Boyer (1984) describes the high school as 'home for many students, a place where it is all right to be young' (p. 529), a potential haven for adolescents to learn about school subjects, their peers, and even the larger world. The teacher's role in this greater community, and its various support systems, is one of the key topics of so-called effective schools research. Without seeking to prove or disprove the accuracy of the effective schools model, it quickly becomes apparent that many of the 'factors' of effectiveness identified by this literature are rooted in collegial cooperation among staff. The most commonly cited factors are: high expectations, an orderly environment or positive school climate, consensus over academic goals, instructional leadership, and frequent, diagnostic assessment. To treat any of these factors successfully, teachers need to work with other staff, frequently over a long period of time, and almost always in arrangements of shared decision-making.

A recent California study of seventy-nine high schools seems to verify some of the findings of effective schools research. At the twenty-one schools which reported the best student performance, researchers found that:

- Faculty and administrators at effective schools shared a common sense of purpose that guided curriculum development and influenced classroom and administrative procedures. At low-performing schools, there often were strong disagreements.
- Teachers at effective schools had designed tests to pinpoint strengths and weaknesses of incoming students, assign the students to appropriate courses, and, after mastery of the targeted skills, permit them to enter the next course in the curriculum sequence. These were not common practices at the low-performance schools.
- At effective schools, faculty reviewed the curriculum regularly and tried to expand it to assure that students received experiences in such subjects as vocational training, art, drama, music, and foreign languages. (California Study Assesses Factors in School Effectiveness, 1984, p. 3)

Thus, the study shows that 'teacher-to-teacher links', as Lieberman

(1984) calls them, significantly enhance the *professional* environment of the school by enabling teachers and administrators to rise above idiosyncratic classroom situations and cultivate the full problem-solving capacity of the institution as a whole. It is interesting to note that the the California experience seems to be mindful, too, of the characteristics of individual students and the needs of particular groups of students.

One can arrive at the same argument for greater teacher participation in schoolwide problem-solving by routes other than the effective schools factors. Cuban (1984) and Peterson (1983) contend that neither research nor centralized authorities should define good teaching practices and effective school administration. Cuban, in particular, warns of the 'danger of converting correlations into policies' (p. 132). Nevertheless, both writers acknowledge the importance of teachers being problem-solvers. Peterson goes so far as to describe problem-solving as part of a teacher's 'art form' (p. 104). But again, the most effective problem-solving is the result of group participation. Such participation, says Lieberman (1984) promotes teachers' ownership of the process and products of education. Moreover, by taking part in the decisions of the school, whether it be in re-thinking curricula, devising new discipline policies, or determining student assignments and tracking procedures, teachers become valued and contributing members of the faculty and of their profession. The autonomy described by Kamii (1984) and advocated by Etzioni (1982) for the successful student is mirrored in the teacher's intrinsic self-discipline and personal commitment to carrying out his or her calling. This kind of self-sufficiency encompasses interactions not only within the school, but beyond it, to the district level and into the homes and community as well. According to Sizer (1984d), the prestige of the profession may, in fact, hinge on allowing teachers to reach out to the entire school community and on providing them with enough stability of position to carry on their collaborative work over a significant period of time.

The current practice of looking at individual school buildings as units of educational renewal has given impetus to teachers' relatively new role as professional decision-makers. Rutter's (1979) research on how staff members work together successfully in model organizations points up the importance of schools functioning as 'coherent wholes' (p. 192). It also parallels the interest of cognitive psychologists in observing model learners who have achieved exemplary skills and knowledge. Taken together, these two kinds of research imply that good teachers can recognize the characteristics of successful student performance and that the learner's year-by-year progress can be translated into appropriate courses of study. The dilemma now confronting effective schools research is whether such descriptive data can, or even should, be turned into prescriptions for all schools. Similarly, in terms of evaluation, the question is whether standardized measures exist that are equal to the teachers' intuitive grasp or direct observation of students' school progress.

The desirability of collective decision-making has significant implications for building and district policy. It may, for example, change the role of the central office from a directive and evaluative role to one that is more supportive and informative; the role of the principal may change in a like manner. Several of the reform reports deal with principal-teacher relations, district evaluation practices, and rules and regulations affecting classroom responsibility. Working conditions obviously influence a teacher's role, too, and are related to particular views of teaching.

The Conditions of Teachers' Work

There are at least three aspects to examining working conditions in any profession: compensation and rewards, social status, and work responsibilities. Nearly all of the current crop of reform reports, but especially the efficiency-based ones, advocate higher teacher salaries. This comes as no surprise; teachers, when compared to other university-trained professionals, have historically been poorly compensated. But *Horace's Compromise*, for one, doubts whether good teachers take teaching positions only for the pay; it proposes that autonomy and respected responsibility may play a greater role in attracting good teachers to their profession. In fact, in private schools, it suggests, teachers may accept lower pay for better teaching circumstances: 'One speculates that private school teachers have made their peace with chancy poverty and, more important, that they feel more in control of their schools' (p. 181).

Most of the reports go on to recommend that especially good teaching be rewarded in some fashion. *High School* would like to see schools recognize creative teaching by giving teachers the opportunity to visit other schools engaged in particularly novel learning programs. *Educating Americans for the 21st Century* suggests reimbursing teachers for in-service. *Making the Grade* calls for a federally-funded National Master Teachers Program in which teachers could earn as much as

$40,000 per year as distinguished classroom instructors. *A Nation at Risk* and *Action for Excellence* take a different path to improving working conditions. Both of these reports advocate increasing the amount of actual teaching time by making better use of already-scheduled periods and by lengthening the actual school calendar. In contrast, *High School* suggests that countering the negative aspects of bureaucracy, by, for example, eliminating teachers' non-academic responsibilities and freeing them from administrative trivia, may be the more prudent approach to the use of finite instructional time. *High School* also goes to great length to make clear that it is the substance of instruction — not the mere cosmetic of time — that leads to the attainment of real academic gains. Moreover, both *High School* and *Horace's Compromise* advise that reducing class size, especially in secondary school, and decreasing the number of classes teachers must meet each day might produce greater job satisfaction among teaching staff.

Other recommendations in the reports are tied to underlying educational policies. Before a district can institute a master teachers program, it must resolve questions like: How are such teachers selected, by what criteria, and by whom? If teachers are to be compensated for in-service workshops, what kinds of workshops are covered and how accessible is this award to all faculty members? There may be views of supervision and management embedded in recommendations of a particular report. In *High School*, the principal is a leader drawn from the teaching ranks and understanding of the classroom situation. *Horace's Compromise* and *The Paideia Proposal* advocate a principal who is, in fact, a headteacher in the mode similarly characterized by Rutter and his associates (1979). The reform reports reveal some major philosophical divisions in their approaches to the conditions of teachers' work and in their assumptions about the worthiness of that work and how it fits into a larger picture of employment and compensation. McNett (1984) indicates there is a conflict between paying teachers as though they are 'hired hands' and expecting performance from them that is professional in standard. Few of the reports address this conflict with anything other than a suggestion for schools to recruit more competitively in the market-place.

Although the reports touch upon the role of unions in determining teachers' working conditions, for the most part they shy from discussing unions *per se*. The exceptions are *Making the Grade* and *Horace's Compromise*. *Making the Grade* strongly favors using its Master

Teacher Program as a merit award, thus opposing the equal pay position advocated by the country's largest teacher union, the National Education Association. The stance in *Horace's Compromise*, on the other hand, tends to parallel the general union position on collective bargaining. What is necessary in this reform period, it says, is a 'decentralization of substantial authority to the persons close to the students' (p. 195). This view corroborates Johnson's (1984) thesis that a status award like merit pay 'accounts neither for the motivational needs of teachers nor the interdependent nature of schools' (p. 175). The legacy of the reports, it would seem, leaves issues of concern to teachers unions very much in question, as many response articles show (Futrell, 1985; Lieberman, 1985; Finn, 1985).

Assessment of Teachers

Another aspect of working conditions in schools is teacher evaluation. To evaluate a teacher's performance, a consensus must first be reached on the characteristics of a good teacher. Some of those characteristics are suggested by the very problems that are the subjects of reform. According to the various reports, good teachers are masters of their subject matters and of students' learning, especially in cognitive, metacognitive, and motivational areas of development. They are capable of mediating students' learning in the classroom, as well as collaborating in substantive ways with their own colleagues. Good teachers are also natural and trusted leaders in the overall working of a school. Those persons who are able to increase in inner city schools' 'holding power' over potential dropouts are obviously of particular value to large city systems, as are staff members with fluent bilingual ability. Also deserving of the 'good teacher' distinction are middle and junior high school teachers who can inspire an early adolescent youngster's genuine interest in school studies and model for them essential skills. Also needed are high school teachers who can help teenage students relate academic materials to their new young adult concerns, as well as to their future plans for further study of employment.

But evaluating teachers is by no means a simple, short-term process. By what criteria are teachers to be evaluated, by whose authority, and according to what mechanisms? There are those who see the selection and assessment of professional staff as predominantly a school-level responsibility. *Horace's Compromise* calls for self-monitoring, and is very wary of standardized, uniform measures. *The Paideia Proposal* makes hiring and firing personnel the principal's prerogative, but only after he or she consults with faculty representatives. *High School* states that the evaluation of teacher performance 'should be largely controlled by other teachers who themselves have been judged to be outstanding in the classroom' (p. 311). These more equity-individual orientations to evaluation contrast with other reports that call for formal and external teacher assessment. *Educating Americans for the 21st Century* recommends that local boards of education evaluate teachers. *A Nation at Risk* recommends a peer review, 'so that superior teachers can be rewarded, average ones encouraged, and poor ones either improved or terminated' (p. 30). *Action for Excellence*, on the other hand, calls for boards of education, higher education, teachers, and school administrators to jointly develop a totally new 'system for fairly objectively measuring the effectiveness of teachers' (p. 39).

The complexity of issues in evaluating successful teaching is formidable and ranges from unions' discomfort with peer review to the intricacies of state-sponsored teacher competency tests. The only directive is that interested parties need to discuss and sort out the issues. The first and most promising step in this process is to define effective teaching.

The Preparation of Teachers

Teacher preparation and certification is the final area within the context of the profession of teaching that is raised in the eight reform reports. Virtually all the reports want better prepared and assessed teachers, but, as one might expect, the studies vary on what they maintain sound teacher education should be. *A Nation at Risk* emphasizes subject matter knowledge, mainly in the liberal arts, and demonstrated aptitude for teaching. It speaks of tightening admission standards at the undergraduate level and retraining mathematics and science specialists to assume now-vacant teaching positions. *Action for Excellence* calls for better teacher preservice and inservice education programs and looks to state agencies to direct the restructuring of teacher training curricula. Beyond specifying that training programs pay special attention to 'enriched academic knowledge' and the 'management and application of technology', teacher preparation guidelines in *Educating Americans for the 21st Century* are rather vague. The report recommends that state governments develop teacher training and retraining programs in cooperation with colleges and universities, and that immediate federal funds be made available for the science and mathematics portions of these state programs. It also asks that regional training and resource centers be established to help schools in computer instruction, information technologies, and curriculum evaluation.

Surprisingly, two reports have very little to say about formal teacher preparation. The first, *Academic Preparation for College*, seems only to imply that teachers need to know the competency areas or subject matter that is the content of education. The second report, *Making the Grade*, introduces its Master Teachers Program with great flourish but then emphasizes that the program's chief purpose is to keep excellent teachers in the classroom, not necessarily to serve as an incentive for improving their skills. Of the five years of a Master Teacher's tenure, only one would involve professional improvement, perhaps at graduate school. The other four years would be spent at the teacher's original school helping other teachers. The research into the learning process that *Making the Grade* advises involves university personnel, but suggests no role for practitioners in the classroom.

Interestingly, it is Adler, Boyer and Sizer, all members of the Paideia Group, who, to a greater or lesser degree, seem to consider teachers' formal education as an important facet of reform. *The Paideia Proposal* suggests that teacher preparation be made up of a sound academic undergraduate program and a fifth year of specialized training and practice teaching. *High School* is even more specific and outlines a model process for a five-year teacher preparation program:

- Completing a core curriculum rooted in the liberal arts;
- Achieving a cumulative grade point average of B and obtaining teacher recommendations to qualify as a prospective teacher;
- Completing an undergraduate academic discipline major and having some experience in classroom observation;
- Finishing a fifth year program of professional studies; and
- Graduating after ample classroom exposure and teaching experience under careful supervision. (pp. 174–5)

As detailed as this model is, Boyer sees the five-year program as being just one step in the overall teacher education process. Credentialling, says *High School*, should be kept separate from college preparation. For certification, teachers would submit materials to a state licensing office and pass written examinations. In the interest of creating a career ladder for teachers, *High School* recommends that the first two years of employment be spent as an associate teacher working under a mentor-teacher-supervisor or senior teacher. Then, after three years of teaching on their own, teachers would be eligible to become senior teachers. Each new level of the career ladder would be accompanied by increased compensation and status.

Horace's Compromise shares the notion of strong academic undergraduate programs, but doubts that even those programs can provide the general education required of today's teachers. The report counts heavily on a fifth year of study which, it maintains, 'must almost be wholly school-based' (p. 194) and in the coaching mode. In addition, *Horace's Compromise* expresses a very serious concern about the tendency toward specialization in American schooling and the related danger of treating instruction as though it were merely technology. In the end, Sizer is as skeptical about higher education instruction as he is about Horace's performance.

With the exception of *High School*, the reform reports reveal that, at least from their perspective, teacher education is not a particular focus of national anxiety. One cannot help but think it strange that while the reports generally lament the dismal state of education of youth in American society, they connect it to teacher education only in passing. Partly, this may be due to the fact that most of the reports demand quick actions and rapid results, and revamping teacher education is not a speedy solution. Nor is it inexpensive. Nonetheless, there is sizable research to suggest that the key to fundamental, long-range change in American education is in improving the nation's schools of education (Soltis and Timpane, 1984). It is possible that teacher preparation may have the most lasting effects on professional performance.

That there are gaps between universities, colleges, and public schools is widely recognized. That teacher education on university campuses is often marginal and insecure is less talked about but, unfortunately, just as true. Both these situations have implications for the preparation of teachers. The problem is illustrated poignantly by the fact that, through the effective schools research and other investigations over the past decade, some fundamental understandings about the education process have been discovered, but sadly, they are little known in academe. As a result, schools of education, which should be at the forefront of change, lag behind in the knowledge they can present to current and future teachers. Moreover, they lack status on their own campuses to influence instruction or educational research. Some writers call for federal sponsorship of research utilization projects to avoid this kind of knowledge fragmentation (Florio, 1983), and some sponsorship has indeed been initiated, for instance, in recent work of the National

Institute of Education. Others cry that too few resources are being invested in teacher education programs. As serious as both these problems may be, the crux of the matter is that what it takes to prepare a good teacher *is* known and can be made available, with proper support, through teacher education programs. But because most of the reform reports missed the vital relationship of teacher education and professional renewal, the nation generally has failed to rally around better teacher education as a sustained and systematic way to put new ideas into practice. Teacher education, says Fenstermacher (1984), can be an essential base for changing the profession of teaching, if educational leaders enable it to be so.

In addition to the slow spread of new knowledge and the lack of adequate funding, there are other problems that plague teacher education in America. Eisner (1984), for example, cites the prejudice against education and teaching expressed by liberal arts faculties. At the same time, he points out that educators' preference for research models from the social or behavioral sciences often obscures the unique and powerful view that they can draw from actual school settings. This same bias appears in several of the reform reports when they present improving teacher's mastery of liberal arts as the sole means of academic improvement. Eisner also addresses the difficulty in understanding teaching as an *applied* enquiry. Much as *Horace's Compromise* emphasizes school-based learning for teacher preparation, Eisner (1984) stresses that managing complex experiences in the classroom is an art and a holistic craft that must be practiced in context. Other researchers emphasize the need for implementing scientific and technical knowledge in education, stressing the theory rather than the applied practice (Baker, 1984; Reed, 1984). The challenge of building a sound integrated teacher education program looms large. The reform reports may finally move us to demand that education come of age as a full-fledged academic discipline and shed its image as the step-child of America's universities. But much must be done to meet that challenge. Indeed, if this is to be done, educators must:

> ... begin with the assumption that what teaching needs most of all is to develop as a *profession*. Teaching needs a community of people who build and share a body of systematic knowledge about education, who hold and enforce commonly understood standards of ethical behavior in their work, and who therefore guarantee the public against ineffective or harmful teaching. (Soltis and Timpane, 1984, p. 24)

Several new programs for teacher preparation are being proposed in the context of the current reform effort. Soltis and Timpane (1984) present a career-based curriculum similar to that in *High School* which involves collaboration across the university as well as between the college and elementary and secondary schools. They advocate peer review, more emphasis on actual teaching, and differentiated compensation. The Phoenix Agenda, a major teacher education proposal developed by Joyce and Clift (1984), suggests revamping the structure, curriculum, and environment of teacher preparation programs in order to achieve four major improvements:

- increasing academic preparation for teachers;
- building clinical training around functionally important areas that interrelate theory and practice;
- fostering collaborative teaching by school and college personnel; and
- emphasizing post-collegiate preparation through career-long education (pp. 13–14).

Both of these programs respond to many of the issues in the reports. Thinking skills and cognitive process concerns can be made part of the teacher's content and methodological preparation; the needs of urban black and Hispanic students can be examined jointly by university faculty and school district personnel and incorporated into collaborative staff development; concerns about family, child development, and adolescence can be considered in planning for curricula, testing procedures, and guidance practices.

The important thing is to realize that school reform has but opened the door to understanding who is a good teacher. There are still conflicting definitions, different approaches to philosophy, authority, and conditions of performance. Nor do many the reports recognize the significance of teacher education. Nonetheless, it is heartening to see that even the National Commission has finally realized that an in-depth study of teacher preparation is needed (Teacher Education to be Studied by National Commission, 1984; Education School in Midst of Reform, 1984). To quote Feistritzer (1984):

Nothing in American education is in greater need of reform than the way we educate and certify classroom teachers. Higher salaries, status, and prestige for teachers will not be forthcoming until we are much more selective about who we let teach. Teaching will never be a true profession until it adopts 'rites of passage,' selection procedures at the entry level, as well as standards of excellence and competence on the job. (p. 54)

The preparation of teachers as professionals may be the key to educating 'all American elementary and secondary students so that their achievement is the best in the world by 1995' (*Educating Americans for the 21st Century*, 1983 from the title). Missing the point could relegate the current effort at school reform to the dustbin of history.

9 *The Impact of Reform*

Do we have the ingenuity to adapt to the realities of a global economy? Do we have the common sense to adjust our nationalism to a world of technology and science that is totally indifferent to national frontiers? Do we have the wisdom to realize that our fate is inextricably bound up with the fate of all the peoples of the globe? Can we practice a self-interest that is enlightened?

Henry Steele Commager, *Harper's Magazine* (1984)

Assessing the Current Period

The study of any period of reform is apt to raise the question, What difference does it make? The current period is no exception. And yet, there is no easy answer. Like assessing student achievement or the capabilities of teachers, one can be long on rhetoric and short on veracity.

The impact of the present reform period will be judged by how its educational changes hold up over time. Some critics will, no doubt, look to quick action as the main measure of effect. But, if anything, this comparative study shows that the reform recommendations of the eighties raise many more issues than quick solutions. A year after *Action for Excellence* appeared, the National Governors Conference declared that although educational renewal had indeed begun, still more action was necessary to keep the momentum going. Specifically, the governors' report says that teachers and principals must be brought into the reform efforts launched by various states. On another occasion, Florida's Education Commissioner cautioned that too much can happen too fast and this 'can be as destructive as no change at all' (Breckenridge, 1984, p. 7). In assessing educational reform, it is quality of impact in the long-term, not temporary influence, that carries the most weight.

There seems to be a sense that the present reform period is a particularly historic one for American education. David Hamburg (1983), President of the Carnegie Corporation, likens it to the period immediately following the Civil War when land-grant colleges were established, thus setting the course of higher education for the next century. In much the same vein, Commager (1984) reminds us that the Morrill Act in 1862 and the Hatch Act of 1887 were both extensions of Jeffersonian policy in their support for public education, and that both carried with them the same equity-oriented view of schooling that some of the reports advocate today.

> The nation has an interest in the education of all children, each of whom, when an adult, can vote for congressmen and for president, and each of whom, therefore, can legislate for the whole nation, and for posterity. (p. 73)

Along with this sense of historical mission, there is general acceptance that reform will have its moments of conflict and frustration. Failure of various report authors to use all of their resources — *A Nation at Risk* rarely cities its own commissioned papers (see Appendix C) — has garnered much criticism, although in this case, the fault may stem from the difficulty of absorbing such abundant and complex materials within given time constraints. *High School* warns of potential conflict in the delicate balance among national priorities, state guidelines, and local control, a concern validated by recent difficulties over state competency tests in urban districts. To whatever extent such conflicts help clarify educational goals, purposes, and future directions, they have value. Joyce and Clift (1984) see the current period of reform as an opportune time for the educational research community to assert its spirit of inquiry on the implementation of change. But will even that response be 'invariably incremental and piecemeal' (Ravitch, 1983)? Or will there be a fundamental and widespread resolve not to repeat the mistakes of the past? Impact follows from capturing the opportunity of the moment. In this case, it is contingent on how well the arguments in the reform reports are examined and acted upon.

What has this analysis of reform reports told us about American education? This examination leads to many realizations about the complex tasks of schooling a nation. At the least, it should have increased our understanding of education in three distinct ways: as a global issue, as a cultural phenomenon, and in terms of the problems of change inherent in the process of reform itself.

Education as a Global Issue

The reform reports of the eighties were inspired by international competition, especially in high-technical industry. America's economy had begun to feel the pressure of worldwide rivalry for technical competence and profitability in the marketplace. Fears about Japanese outstripping American productivity alerted manufacturers to the need for a capable workforce, especially in areas like mathematics, science, and computer technology. This, in turn, raised questions about American student achievement, particularly in comparison to student achievement in other industrialized societies. Results from comparative research studies indicated that American students often scored lower than those in Japan, Sweden, Israel or France (Husén, 1983; Bridgman, 1984, May; Travers and McKnight, 1985). Whether such tests are accurate assessments of a country's educational system is a point of dispute among researchers (Stedman and Smith, 1983; Hurn, 1983). Recent international test findings, however, seem to indicate that various kinds of information can, indeed, emanate from such cross-cultural comparisons (Coleman, 1985; Jacobson and Doran, 1985).

The global nature of educational competition is only now becoming understood. More and more countries are recognizing that how they academically prepare their youth has national and international consequences. British educators worry about West German accomplishments in mathematics (Hechinger, 1984); Russian leaders are recognizing the need for early childhood education and vocational preparation (Kimelman, 1984); Japan's Ministry of Education, concerned about developing fifth generation computers, is exploring how to develop creative researchers in technical fields (Lohr, 1984); and in Venezuela, the former Minister for the Development of Human Intelligence has written a book on the importance of every child's right to think (Machado, 1980). But examining education as a global phenomenon raises the question: How are educational standards established in a particular society? How important is formal testing? What influence do particular groups hold over subject matter, or basic research, or the processes of learning? How do graduation requirements influence college admission? How does university training influence employment? The international comparisons in the reform

127

reports touch upon many of these issues but never seriously explore them. Partially because there are few cross-cultural examinations actually available. One recent study of American, Japanese, and Taiwanese students by Stevenson (Fiske, 1984; Irwin, 1984) suggests national differences actually appear quite early in elementary school. Stevenson's research implies that a K–12 study, or multiple year performance, is really required to conduct sound international comparisons. This seems to be corroborated in Coleman's (1985) review of the second international study of cognitive achievement.

What this global concern shows is complexity in instruction is much more than a technical matter. It is a historical and cultural matter as well. Education in Japan is a prime example of historical adaptation. Prior to World War II, Japan was still a near-feudal society. Caste and class determined a person's life and education. After the war, in seeking to democratize the country, the United States gave its assistance wherever necessary. That is why, to some extent, the evolution of Japan's schools has been an American success story. New curricula, new teaching methods, and new emphases for instruction in an industrialized society revolutionized Japan's centuries-old educational system and made it an international showcase (Ranbom, 1985). One recent report (Harper's Index, 1984) indicates Japanese adults score above 130 on standardized IQ tests five times more frequently than do Americans. Whether Japan's educational system is better than America's and better for whom, is a cultural question: Do Japan's schools foster what the Japanese people want to become *as a society*? Using the Japanese as a mirror, not as a model, leads to the question: As a nation, what does the United States want schools to prepare youngsters to be? That is the real issue that emerges from comparing the reform reports of the eighties. The international dimension leads to an appraisal of American's own cultural perspective.

Education and American Culture

A society's values determine the kinds of institutions and programs upon which that society thrives. Several key values shape American society, and the reform reports reflect what those values mean in our culture. Utility is one key value. Americans appreciate things that are useful and practical. Education can be considered in this same light because 'it provides skills and advances careers' (Hurn, 1983, p. 10). Part of America's anti-intellectualism comes from associating esoteric knowledge with 'ivory tower' or impractical learning. Conversely, in European tradition, the prestige accorded intellectual life parallels its degree of non-utility. Hurn (1983) cites the famous toast at Cambridge University in the 1930s: 'To pure mathematics, may it never be of use to anyone!' (p. 10). By and large, such thinking would be very unAmerican. There is a second value of consequence in American society that has to do with who controls what knowledge. Americans are highly committed to egalitarianism. They treasure an open society. The benefits of society should be available to every citizen of the Republic on an equal basis. That is, in effect, the highest utility. The educational and cultural elites of Old World society are essentially anathema to American schooling. Finally, still a third value appears frequently in American society — the importance of the individual, the single citizen whose human rights are described in and protected by the Constitution. Every individual must learn, and the needs of every individual must be incorporated into the design of instruction. How are these three key values treated in the current reform reports?

Unsurprisingly, the eight reports differ in how their writers perceive these basic American values and how they treat them in both open and hidden assumptions. Efficiency-based studies tend to empha-size the utilitarian dimensions of schooling: using time well; preparing students for jobs; and developing state guidelines, plans, and testing procedures to produce solid, educational products. On one hand, such utilitarianism is very American. One recent presidential advisory panel suggests, 'education of the citizenry must strive for standards of excellence compatible with the effective functioning of this republic' (Advisory Panel on Financing Elementary and Secondary Education, 1982, p. 1). One the other hand, this position leads to other questions, as the reports themselves acknowledge, which are related to egalitar-ianism and individualism, both equity issues. How can we have an education system that is efficient and utilitarian in a national sense, and at the same time, serves local concerns and the idiosyncratic needs of a heterogeneous population? What, in fact, does education mean to the culture of America?

That education is primarily a state responsibility is a given — by default — of the Constitution. The United States has no uniform national curriculum, no national examination of students, no national standards for the certification of teachers. The Scholastic Achievement Test and the National Assessment of Educational Progress are rare instances of national assessment and they are much less formidable than testing programs in countries such as Japan or France. Americans prize their alternative, creative approaches to education. This attitude is, perhaps, an extension of Yankee ingenuity. Americans also hold in high esteem voluntary participation in activities. In the United States, parents send their children to school because they want them to have an education, not because the law requires them to do so. Unlike many European schools or those in Japan, American schools stress the intrinsic motivation for learning rather than student allegiance or the subordination of the learner to the authority of the school.

American culture, it seems, places a heavy emphasis on the *will* of the individual to learn and the committed motivation of a student who seeks personalized and idiosyncratic meaning in his or her life. This general spirit of individualism and equity pervades all the reform documents, but as a cultural value is portrayed differently in the various reports. *Horace's Compromise* cites 'the hungry student'; *The Paideia Proposal* speaks of every student's 'drive to learn'; *A Nation at Risk* emphasizes deportment and character development above content. Where differences appear in the reports is where this value confronts the new industrialism and the higher order skills of modern science, mathematics, and computer technology.

There is a disquieting impression in this reform period as in all prior reform periods, that begs the question: Are things different now? If American citizens are to be ready for the high-tech world, does our educational system have to change dramatically? In spite of Stedman and Smith's (1983) finding that jobs of the future will require relatively low skills, aren't the academic competencies — such as suggested in *Academic Preparation for College* — of prime importance to all students? There is a nagging fear behind this question that none of the reports really articulated, but has been posed by others. Torsten Husén, the Swedish researcher involved in international assessment, asks whether schools — particularly in a technologically sophisticated society — can continue to serve as equalizers in that society. The role of equalizer has, of course, been played by American schools since the time of Horace Mann. Husén (1983) answers the question negatively. He argues that learning today, especially in technical and sequential content material 'establishes, reinforces, and legitimizes differences' (p. 461). Because of this, he suggests, American schooling will have to alter its goals. Naturally, this is a difficult dilemma for American education; a challenge not just to our pedagogical beliefs, but also to our cultural and political ideology. Past reform efforts struggled with this same issue and never resolved the conflict of equity and excellence. The major impact of the reform documents today is that this dilemma is once again revisited. Not only schooling, but America's value orientation is being put to the test. The comparison Hamburg makes between the current reform period and the Civil War era may be fitting indeed.

The reform reports tend to divide between those that treat the current period as a time to sharpen standards, focus on content, locate better teachers and pay them more generously; and those reports that stress the importance of good teaching, the motivation of all students, and the development of capability in various subjects by both teachers and students. One approach makes economic goals of business and industry paramount; the other accentuates the cultural goals of a free society. Obviously, an essential task of this reform period is to join these divergent approaches in a single unified thrust. The three problems addressed here — thinking and schooling, understanding student needs, and the profession of teaching — are central, emergent problems in initiating that task. They also lead to any larger understandings about school reform itself that may be concluded from a comparative study. What might these understandings be?

The reform reports spend much time discussing good teaching and the purposes of education in a larger context. Understanding both topics in a cultural context is essential to school reform. Teaching, as both an art and a science, may be closer to parenting than to any other human endeavor. It shares with parents the challenge to model intelligent behaviors at the same time that one focuses on actions to guide performance and execution. The interaction of the teacher and the taught is particularly prominent in the approach to schooling that emphasizes the development of cultural goals. As is happening in other professions, teachers are becoming more and more involved in making decisions that affect the life of the total school. In fact, there is ample research to show that successful change efforts may only be possible when teachers' voluntary cooperation is obtained and when their professional concerns are addressed (Cuban, 1982; Ravitch, 1983).

But there are other considerations looming on the educational horizon, too. How do schools prepare children to become independent and fully able to use the human symbolic capacities available in American culture? Educators are grappling with the question of how symbolic knowledge can best be made available to all learners. Husén (1985) asks, can we have a meritocracy in which all students are players? This particular period, it seems, is a time of great technologial development when the cultural symbols themselves are being transformed. Gardner ((1983) wants us to consider 'multiple intelligences' when examining the capacities of learners and Olsen (1973 and 1976) suggests that decisions about which curricula and instructional methods best present and apply symbolic knowledge are not made easily. The reform reports address these issues in discussing the contents of learning, but only the reports sensitive to education as a product of *cultural exchange embedded in teaching* explore the issue in depth. The links between the teacher, the subject matter, and the learner are forged by such intricate understandings. They are the dynamic ingredients of the culture itself.

There is a growing awareness, too, that schooling is a particular human exchange that needs to become more personalized. Shanker (1984) speaks of education as society's 'human infra-structure.' Larson (1983) discusses Sarason's research on the ethos of the school, also a topic of Rutter's (1979) research, and finds parallels in Goodlad's work as well as in *High School* and *The Paideia Proposal*. The key to establishing a community of scholarship and shared interest in learning is motivating and setting expectations for an individual's school success. Doyle and Cooper (1983) identify urban high schools that have achieved far beyond what has normally come to be expected under seemingly difficult conditions. What has made these rare schools successful is a set of clear goals for academic performance and the ability to inspire each and every student to achieve those goals. This dual emphasis on goals and personalized inspiration seems to be particularly important for the adolescent learner who needs to know what knowledge of most worth and which cognitive processes are the most powerful, and then be motivated to attain both (Presseisen, 1982). It is this faith in the potential of each young person that leads American educators to say:

> Tomorrow's creative genius in mathematics may come out of proper white suburbia, but could well come from backwoods Appalachia or the Hispanic quarter of Los Angeles or anywhere in between. (Best, 1984, p. 272)

Such faith is the talisman of American culture.

And finally, there are questions without exact answers. How much diversity can a society sustain in its educational system? The answer is unknown. Nonetheless, chances are that heterogenous populations who are motivated to succeed do so. The unusual success of Asian-American immigrants is a recent phenomenon discussed frequently in the reform literature (Rubin, 1983; Kaufman, 1984). Success stories of disadvantaged individuals more often than not point to special motivating experiences that encouraged achievement (Williams, 1984). Can we actually *develop* academic prowess? Maybe. Older educational philosophies assumed genius is only a God-given talent. Current theory suggests that may not be the case (Gardner, 1983; Sternberg, 1981). A controversial thesis recently proposed in the field of science suggests that scientific theory moves forward not on the insights of great minds but rather on the improved techniques of many researchers who are able to try out and tinker with new technology (Broad, 1984). Questions about diversity and development of academic achievement make for interesting discussion about students' ability to obtain and use new materials and ideas. They offer an interesting comparison of the United States with the Soviet Union, which discourages its citizens from acquiring or using personal computers, and is seen as 'discouraging originality in industrial products and processes' (Shabad, 1984, p. 4).

Culturally, then, the current reform period has to challenge Husén's argument about the meaning of education in American society. The competitiveness of the contemporary industrial scene and the growing complexities of scientific, mathematical, and technological innovations make it imperative that excellence and equity be equally served. The battle may be hardest to wage in urban high schools, but there is an optimism inherent in American society that says even this arena can be won. Doyle and Cooperman (1983) say that the high achievement they found in the boroughs of New York, could occur anywhere: 'Intelligence and motivation are randomly distributed in the population, and neither New York City nor its special schools has a corner on it' (p. 25). It is the values of egalitarianism and individualism in educational practices, as stressed in *High School*, *Horace's Compromise*, and *Educating Americans for the 21st Century* that, in the long run, may be the most influential aspect of the current reform reports. These documents underscore, as does the larger literature, that the greatest problem facing American society is showing that we treasure our children (Bakalis quoted in Sevener, 1984; Lapham, 1984). Such awareness parallels America's growing consciousness of child abuse and teenage suicide and our new-found sensitivity to the homeless. Providing good education for all children in a democratic Republic may be the highest form of expressing that human value. Commager (1984) might have a lesson in American history for Professor Husén: America's strength is built upon seeking virtue in the common people. We must build our public schools so that education provided there enables all to achieve. Only then will we have a society based on enlightened self-interest.

The Process of Reform

A third consideration in estimating the impact of reform relates to the problems of change inherent in the reform process itself. Assuming the current reevaluation of education leads to a clarification of America's goals and to a consensus on the characteristics of good teaching, how do we proceed?

One of the first steps in implementing reform is to build what Goodlad (1983) calls 'the necessary coalition of contributing groups' (p. 293). This means identifying and coordinating the various parties who play a role in school improvement. The many task forces, commissions, and special committees will all come to naught if they do not reach out and induce the formal educational enterprise to act. Among professional educators, there are different functions that need to be fulfilled at local, state, and federal levels. Passow (1984) suggests these leaders must examine their own policies and practices while simultaneously coordinating their improvement efforts with other levels in the system.

Second, learning more about how educational systems actually change must be given a high priority if schools are to improve. Recent research on hasty, ill-planned programs shows the importance of carefully thought out implementation strategies to improvement success (Purkey, 1984). Crandall (1984) proposes a major two-prong system of improvement that involves both short and long-term strategies. His changes affect different parties in various ways and alter many relationships in the present system. What are the consequences of these changes for relationships between unions and school boards, or for the roles of administrators and teachers? Reforms should not be pursued if changes do not work toward more effective institutions, yet that is no simple outcome to deliver.

Third, the task of implementing change must reach beyond formal educational networks. Numerous studies cite the need for more family involvement in the education of children (Farrer, Neufeld and Miles, 1984; Irwin, 1984). Generating interest in the community-at-large is another often cited approach (Shreeve *et al.*, 1984; Seeley, 1984). Since black and Hispanic groups are under-represented in urban politics generally, their involvement in community institutions like schools is also low. Yet, their support is essential to school improvement. And finally, it will be necessary to arouse interest in reform among the many professional associations that touch school personnel. Linkages across communities, between states, and throughout the country are vital if improvement is to influence our national educational enterprise. The recent attention given to reform in entire journal issues such as *Daedalus* (Graubard, 1984, Fall), *Education and Urban Society* (Ginsberg and Wimpelberg, 1985), and the *LRE Project Exchange* (Naylor, 1985) needs to be extended.

A fourth step in implementing reform involves developing and institutionalizing leadership for educational change. Some see this task as an appropriate role for teacher education institutions and higher education in general (Fenstermacher, 1984; Joyce and Clift, 1984). Others see it as the task for principals or chief state school officers. *Educating Americans for the 21st Century* and *Making the Grade* call for a federally-sponsored leadership through government channels to reach formally across the entire nation. Whoever assumes this responsibility must be willing to pursue the grittiest problems facing school reform, 'to deal with the major gaps and unattended issues left on their agendas in the wake of the reports and studies' (Howe, 1983, p. 168). Student dropout, especially in urban schools; unemployment among black and Hispanic youth; the increased costs of improving education; and the retooling of existing staffs are only the beginning of a long list of problems that cry out for immediate attention. And, just as important, whoever takes on this leadership position must be able to sustain an enthusiasm for reform long after the reports themselves have been forgotten.

Last, and very practically, educational reform cannot progress without financial resources. People, time, and materials are necessary costs that are not considered to any great degree in most of the reform reports. The efficiency reports want more outcome for no greater cost, perhaps forgetting that additional school time and increased teacher salaries are costly items for all school districts. Lieberman (1984) warns that school improvements cannot really be sustained unless collective bargaining agreements become part of the total improvement effort. Multi-year projects leading to successful improvements in city schools, as were recently reported by the Ford Foundation (1984), translate into formidable budgets over extended periods of time. The high cost of installing up-to-date computer technology underscores the expensiveness of modern, quality education. There are ways to determine both low-cost and high-cost strategies in educational improvement, says Odden (1984), and he suggests we immediately pursue the low cost options so that good will can be built 'to help weather future tradeoffs necessitated by finite resources' (p. 318).

There are some promising developments on the horizon that

indicate even the cost of change may not deter reform efforts. Inexpensive materials are appearing that help school districts evaluate their own studies of district policies and procedures (Spady and Marx, 1984; Dianda, 1984). Teacher salaries are rising across the nation and business and industry, for the first time in American history, is spending more money on research and development than does the federal government (Boffey, 1984). The Ford Foundation recently earmarked a significant portion of its grant monies for projects assisting Hispanics, including research on educational attainment (Ford to nearly double program support, 1984). There is hope that other prospects for funding the nation's schools in their effort to reform will just as generously come to fruition. If, for no other reason, the 37 per cent increase in demand for kindergarten and elementary teachers expected by 1995 should induce current school reform (500,000 More Teachers to be Needed, 1984). The nation needs success in these endeavors.

Looking back at nearly a hundred years of school reform, one can say that particular historic periods have indeed made a difference. They hold up a mirror in which the country can examine the image of its educational enterprise. They provide a brief opportunity to improve the reflection of the nation's inner self.

Epilogue

Periods of reform need not be periods of 'exaggerated breast-beating and invidious comparisons' (Hurn, 1983, p. 12). Such times encourage examination of what has happened and assessment of what was expected and desired. Lazerson (1985) warns educators to be careful of memory's distortion and to be aware of the tendency to think of the past as a golden age when, in reality, many things, including schools, were tarnished already then. He reminds us, 'some of the most difficult dilemmas we currently face have been around for a long time' (p. 32).

One of the most significant aspects of an educational reform period is its ability to develop perspective on complex issues that underlie schooling. Comparing several reform periods enables us to examine different visions of education. Reaching back to the documents of nearly a century ago and contrasting them to a new set of recommendations for America's schools helps us see where we are going in terms of where we have been. How we mentally construct that examination can be very compelling.

Historian Carl Kaestle suggests that the metaphor of the swinging pendulum is an inadequate description of American educational reform. The conflict between periods that stress standards and academic achievement and times when students' interests or humanitarian concerns rise to the surface does not depict reality in America's vast educational system. Kaestle (1985) likens education to a sailing vessel, pressed upon by varying conditions and contexts, but not really changing that much or that fast:

> The real U.S. school system is more like a huge tanker going down the middle of a channel, rocking a bit from side to side as it attends to one slight current and then to another. (p. 423)

The important question is where the ship is heading, what destination it seeks, and what conditions influence the quality of the voyage *en route*? Reform periods are times to consider and select options that might influence the ship's destiny.

There are those educational commentators who believe America today is at a particular turning point in the development of its schools. Some are concerned with backlash and the retreat from democracy (Finkelman 1984; Graubard, 1984; Toch, 1985). Others like Holton (1984) maintain that the potential for strong and long-lasting action exists, but conflicting directives can lead down several paths. The main motivation behind the efficiency reports is to remove the federal presence, introduce religious and other private concerns, and increase local and corporate activity in pre-collegiate education. The equity and excellence-oriented reports seek to enhance the ability of our younger citizens, especially in expanding technological subject areas, by capitalizing on the success of meaningful and effective teaching relationships. Much of what these two visions involve depends on where their advocates think American education has been over the last century.

Three vignettes present different perspectives on education — dissimilar views on authority, the role of the teacher, the place of schooling in society, and the significance of education to individual development. In a way, these vignettes capture the essence of historic reform and show how reform periods exist along a continuum of development and change:

- A letter to the *New York Times* reviewed an addendum to a teacher's wage agreement in New York's Sullivan County in 1910, about half-way between the Report of the Committee of Ten and the publication of *The Cardinal Principles*:

    Teachers are expected to keep the schoolroom clean and neat at all times by:

    (a) Sweeping the floors at least once each day.
    (b) Scrubbing the floor once each week with hot water and lye soap.
    (c) Cleaning the blackboards daily.
    (d) Starting the fire at 7 a.m. so that the school room will be warm by 8 a.m.

    Teachers will not dress in bright colors. Dresses must not be more than two inches above the ankles. At least two petticoats must be worn. Their petticoats will be dried in pillowcases.

Teachers will not marry, or keep company with men, during the terms of her [sic] employment.

She will not get into a carriage, or automobile, with any man, except her brother or father. Teachers will not loiter at ice cream stores.

Teachers are expected to be at home between the hours of 8 p.m. and 6 a.m. unless in attendance at a school function.

The teacher will not smoke cigarets or play at cards. She will not dye her hair under any circumstance.

It is understood the teacher will attend church each Sunday and either teach a class in Sunday School or sing in the choir.

The teacher will not leave town at any time without permission of the Chairman of the School Board. (Feldman, 1984, p. 22E)

- A recent discussion between a journal editor-historian and a major foundation executive about the funding of prospective research reveals some deep-seated feelings about education:

When asked to support a study of three contemporary professions — law, medicine, and teaching — he found the idea laughable. Law and medicine, he explained rather grandly, deserved the dignity of being called a profession; teaching was not a profession at all. What, then, was it? Gazing out from his windows high over vast expanses of New York, he intoned: 'Teachers resemble other city workers; they are like police, firemen', and then, with deliberate emphasis and a calculated pause, '— garbage collectors'. Should remarks of this sort be dismissed as the jaundiced view of an individual disillusioned with city schools, influenced perhaps by mass-media accounts of school conditions, or ought it to be understood as a balanced grievance against those teachers who, more than a decade ago, took to the streets, went out on strike, finding no other solution to their problems? Is the comment to be read more as a statement about one foundation executive, his prejudices and beliefs, possibly idiosyncratic, than about the objective conditions that exist in one of our country's major cities? Perhaps. (Graubard, 1984, p. 87)

• In 1984, John Goodlad in *A Place Called School* proposed a four-part transformation of the teacher's responsibility as a way to address major problems of schooling:

> This would be to reduce the instructional time of teachers to approximately 15 hours per week (as in Japan) — the top teaching load at colleges and universities — while simultaneously initiating school-based programs of curricular and instructional improvement shared by the entire staff. First, teachers presumably could teach, as one might hope, for three hours each day. Second, the curricular deficiencies discussed ... could be addressed, simultaneously providing for teachers an intellectual challenge now largely missing (and proving linkages to subject-matter specialists and behavioral scientists in universities). Third, professional staff development could be built into the work week, as it is at the college and university level. Fourth, the need to provide for children and youths beyond what schools can do best would provide an urgency regarding the use of nonformal and informal educational resources of the entire community. (p. 194)

How different these three worlds. It is hard to believe they describe the same society or the same educational system. What do they reveal about our understanding of education at the close of the twentieth century? Americans have a great deal to consider in this time of educational reform. There are many complex problems to resolve. We should be wary of returning to an earlier philosophy of Social Darwinism merely to survive. And we should allot more of our energies to examine and use the findings of our own research about schools and schooling.

Comparing reform reports teaches us by the historic record that the progress of American education over the last century, although problematic, has been far from mediocre. This realization should inspire us to meet the multiple challenges of our future with a new enthusiasm.

Appendix A: Four Alternate Programs for College Entrance Specified by the Committee of Ten (1893)

1 *Classical*		2 *Latin-Scientific*	
Three foreign languages (one modern)		Two foreign languages (one modern)	

Year			
I Latin	5p.	Latin	5p.
English	4p.	English	4p.
Algebra	4p.	Algebra	4p.
History	4p.	History	4p.
Physical geography	3p.	Physical geography	3p.
	20p.		20p.
II Latin	5p.	Latin	5p.
English	2p.	English	2p.
German[1] (or French) begun	4p.	German (or French) begun	4p.
Geometry	3p.	Geometry	3p.
Physics	3p.	Physics	3p.
History	3p.	Botany or zoology	3p.
	20p.		20p.
III Latin	4p.	Latin	4p.
Greek[1]	5p.	English	3p.
English	3p.	German (or French)	4p.
German (or French)	4p.	Mathematics (Algebra 2 — Geometry 2)	4p.
Mathematics (Algebra 2 — Geometry 2)	4p.	Astronomy ½ yr. and Meteorology ½ yr.	3p.
	20p.	History	2p.
			20p.

141

IV	Latin	4p.	Latin	4p.
	Greek	5p.	English (as in Classical 2 additional 2)	4p.
	English	2p.		
	German (or French)	3p.	German (or French)	3p.
	Chemistry	3p.	Trigonometry and higher algebra	3p.
	Trigonometry and higher algebra		or	
	or		History	3p.
	History	3p.	Geology or physiography ½ yr; and Anatomy, physiology and hygiene ½ yr.	3p.
		20p.		
				20p.

3 *Modern Languages*		4 *English*	
Two foreign languages (both modern)		One foreign language (both modern)	

Year

I	French (or German) begun	5p.	Latin, or German, or French	5p.
	English	4p.	English	4p.
	Algebra	4p.	Algebra	4p.
	History	4p.	History	4p.
	Physical geography	3p.	Physical geography	3p.
		20p.		20p.

II	French (or German)	4p.	Latin, or German, or French	5 or 4p.
	English	2p.	English	3 or 4p.
	German (or French) begun	5p.	Geometry	3p.
	Geometry	3p.	Physics	3p.
	Physics	3p.	History	3p.
	Botany or zoology	3p.	Botany or zoology	3p.
		20p.		20p.

III	French (or German)	4p.	Latin, or German, or French	4p.
	English	3p.	English (as in other 3 additional 2)	5p.
	German (or French)	4p.		
	Mathematics (Algebra 2 Geometry 2)	4p.	Mathematics (Algebra 2 Geometry 2)	4p.
	Astronomy ½ yr. and Meteorology ½ yr.	3p.	Astronomy ½ yr. and Meteorology ½ yr.	3p.
	History	2p.	History (as in the Latin Scientific 2 additional 2)	4p.
		20p.		
				20p.

IV French (or German)	3p.	Latin, or German, or French	4p.
English (as in Classical, additional 2)	4p.	English (as in Classical additional 2)	4p.
German (or French)	4p.	Chemistry	3p.
Chemistry	3p.	Trigonometry and higher algebra	3p.
Trigonometry and higher algebra *or* History	3p.	History	3p.
		Geology or physiography ½ yr. and.	3p.
Geology or physiography ½ yr. and	3p.	Anatomy, physiology and hygiene ½ yr.	3p.
Anatomy, physiology, and hygiene ½ yr.	3p.		———
	———		20p.
	20p.		

---

1 In any school in which Greek can be better taught than a modern language, or in which local public opinion or the history of the school makes it desirable to teach Greek in an ample way, Greek may be substituted for German or French in the second year of the classical programme.

Source: 'The Committee of Ten — Proposals for a Program for Secondary Schools,' *Report of the Committee of Ten on Secondary School Studies,* Washington, D.C.: United States Bureau of Education, 1893, pp. 46–7.

Appendix B: Participants On Each Panel or Commission of Reports Reviewed

The National Commission on Excellence in Education

David P. Gardner (Chair)
President
University of Utah and President-
  Elect, University of California
Salt Lake City, Utah

Yvonne W. Larsen (Vice-Chair)
Immediate Past-President
San Diego City School Board
San Diego, California

William O. Baker
Chairman of the Board (Retired)
Bell Telephone Laboratories
Murray Hill, New Jersey

Anne Campbell
Former Commissioner of Education
State of Nebraska
Lincoln, Nebraska

Emeral A. Crosby
Principal
Northern High School
Detroit, Michigan

Charles A. Foster, Jr.
Immediate Past-President
Foundation for Teaching Economics
San Franciso, California

Robert V. Haderlein
Immediate Past-President
National School Boards Association
Girard, Kansas

Gerald Holton
Millinckrodt Professor of Physics and
  Professor of the History of Science
Harvard University
Cambridge, Massachusetts

Annette Y. Kirk
Kirk Associates
Mecosta, Michigan

Margaret S. Marston
Member
Virginia State Board of Education
Arlington, Virginia

Albert H. Quie
Former Governor
State of Minnesota
St. Paul, Minnesota

Francisco D. Sanchez, Jr.
Superintendent of Schools
Albuquerque Public Schools
Albuquerque, New Mexico

Norman C. Francis
President
Xavier University of Louisiana
New Orleans, Louisiana

Glenn T. Seaborg
University Professor of Chemistry
    and Nobel Laureate
University of California
Berkeley, California

A. Bartlett Giamatti
President
Yale University
New Haven, Connecticut

Jay Sommer
National Teacher of the Year,
    1981–1982
Foreign Language Department
New Rochelle High School
New Rochelle, New York

Shirley Gordon
President
Highline Community College
Midway, Washington

Richard Wallace
Principal
Lutheran High School East
Cleveland Heights, Ohio

The Paideia Group

Mortimer J. Adler Chairman
    Director, Institute for
    Philosophical Research
Chairman, Board of Editors
Encyclopaedia Britannica

Jacques Barzun
Former Provost, Columbia
University;
Literary Adviser
Charles Scribner's Sons

Otto Bird
Former Head
Generel Program of Liberal Studies
University of Notre Dame

Leon Botstein
President
Bard College

Ernest Boyer
President
Carnegie Foundation for the
    Advancement of Teaching

Nicholas Caputi
Principal
Skyline High School
Oakland, California

Douglass Cater
Senior Fellow
Aspen Institute for Humanistic
    Studies

Donald Cowan
Former President
University of Dallas
Fellow, Dallas Institute of
    Humanities and Culture

Alonzo Crim
Superintendent of Schools
Atlanta, Georgia

Clifton Fadiman
Director
Council for Basic Education

146

Ernest L. Boyer
President
Carnegie Foundation for the
Advancement of Teaching

Lawrence A. Cremin
President
Teachers College
Columbia University

Alonzo Crim
Superintendent of Schools
Atlanta City Schools

William R. Dill
President
Babson College

Nell P. Eurich
Senior Consultant
Academy for Educational
Development

Daniel J. Evans
President
Evergreen State College

Norman C. Francis
President
Xavier University of Louisiana

Stanley O. Ikenberry
President
University of Illinois

Leslie Koltai
Chancellor
Los Angeles Community College
District

Barbara Uehling
Chancellor
University of Missouri, Columbia

Mary Patterson McPherson
President
Bryn Mawr College

Frank Newman
President
University of Rhode Island

Robert M. O'Neil
President
University of Wisconsin

Alan Pifer
President Emeritus and Senior
Consultant
Carnegie Corporation of New York

Lauren B. Resnick
Co-Director, Learning Research and
Development Center
University of Pittsburgh

Frank H.T. Rhodes
President
Cornell University

Tomas Rivera
Chancellor
University of California, Riverside

George L. Shinn
Chairman of the Board
First Boston Corporation

Virginia B. Smith
President
Vassar College

Members of the National High School Panel
(The Carnegie Foundation)

Myron Atkin
Dean, School of Education
Stanford University

Beverly Joyce Bimes
St. Louis, Missouri

Derek Bok
President
Harvard University

Anne Campbell
Commissioner of Education
Lincoln, Nebraska

Joan Ganz Cooney
President
Children's Television Workshop

Lawrence A. Cremin
President
Teachers College
Columbia University

James R. Gaddy
Principal
New Rochelle High School
New Rochelle, New York

Peggy Hanrahan
Principal
Mentor High School
Mentor, Ohio

Leslie Koltai
Chancellor
Los Angeles Community College
    District

Marigold Linton
Professor of Psychology
University of Utah

Alonzo Crim
Superintendent of Schools
Atlanta City Schools

Walter Cronkite
CBS News

Emeral A. Crosby
Principal
Northern High School
Detroit, Michigan

Patrick L. Daly
Vice President
American Federation of Teachers

Norman Francis
President
Xavier University of Louisiana

Mary Hatwood Futrell
Secretary/Treasurer
National Education Association

Alan Pifer
President Emeritus, Senior
    Consultant
Carnegie Corporation of New York

Lauren Resnick
Co-Director
Learning Research & Development
    Center
University of Pittsburgh

Tomás Rivera
Chancellor
University of California, Riverside

Adele Simmons
President
Hampshire College

William A. Marcussen
Vice President
Atlantic Richfield Company

Virginia V. Sparling
President
National Parent & Teachers
   Association

Ralph McGee
Principal
New Trier East Township School
Winnetka, Illinois

Robert R. Wheeler
Superintendent of Schools
Kansas City, Missouri, Schools

James L. Olivero
Project Leadership Executive
Professional Development Program
   Association of California

W. Willard Wirtz
Wirtz and LaPointe

Rayma C. Page
President
National School Boards Association
   and
Chairman, Lee County School Board
Fort Myers, Florida

Daniel Yankelovich
Yankelovich, Skelly, and White, Inc.

Educational EQuality Project, The College Board

George H. Hanford
President

Adrienne Y. Bailey
Vice President for Academic Affairs

Task Force on Education for Economic Growth

Chair

The Honorable James B. Hunt, Jr.
Governor of North Carolina

Co-Chairs

Frank T. Cary
Chairman of the Executive
   Committee
IBM Corporation

The Honorable Pierre S. duPont IV
Governor of Delaware

Governors

The Honorable Lamar Alexander
Governor of Tennessee

The Honorable D. Robert Graham
Governor of Florida

The Honorable Thomas Kean
Governor of New Jersey

The Honorable Richard D. Lamm
Governor of Colorado

The Honorable Scott M. Matheson
Governor of Utah

The Honorable George Nigh
Governor of Oklahoma

The Honorable Robert D. Orr
Governor of Indiana

The Honorable Rudy Perpich
Governor of Minnesota

The Honorable Charles S. Robb
Governor of Virginia

The Honorable Richard L.
   Thornburgh
Governor of Pennsylvania

The Honorable William F. Winter
Governor of Mississippi

State Legislators

The Honorable Wilhelmina Delco
State Representative of Texas

The Honorable Anne Lindeman
State Senator of Arizona

The Honorable Oliver Ocasek
State Senator of Ohio

Business Leaders

Thornton F. Bradshaw
Chairman, RCA Corporation and
   Chairman, Conference Board

J. Fred Bucy
President, Texas Instruments

Philip Caldwell
Chairman of the Board and Chief
   Executive Officer, Ford Motor Co.

James Campbell
President, MISSCO Corporation;
   and Chairman, Education
   Employment and Training
   Comittee, U.S. Chamber of
   Commerce

John H. Johnson
President, Johnson Publishing Co.

David T. Kearns
President and Chief Executive
   Officer
Xerox Corporation; and Member,
   Business Round Table

Robert W. Lundeen
Chairman of the Board, The Dow
   Chemical Company; and Trustee
   Committee for Economic
   Development

Unlearned Lessons

J. Richard Munro
President and Chief Executive
  Officer
Time, Inc.

William C. Norris
Chairman of the Board and Chief
  Executive Officer, Control Data
  Corporation

Bernard J. O'Keefe
Chairman and Chief Executive
  Officer
EG and G, Inc; and Chairman
National Association of
  Manufacturers

James E. Olson
Vice Chairman, Board of Directors
American Telephone and Telegraph
  Company

John R. Purcell
Chairman, Chief Executive Officer
  and President, SFN Companies,
  Inc.

Robert D. Ray
President, Life Investors, Inc.

Labor

Glenn E. Watts
President
Communications Workers of America

Educators

Bruce Brombacher
Teacher of the Year, Jones Junior
  High School
Upper Arlington, Ohio

Dr. Calvin M. Frazier
Commissioner of Education
Colorado

Dr. William C. Friday
President
University of North Carolina

Marvin O. Koenig
Principal
Southwest High School
St. Louis, Missouri

Dr. Floretta McKenzie
Superintendent of Schools
District of Columbia

Judith Moyers
Education Specialist
New York, New York

Organization Leaders

Ms. Joanne T. Goldsmith
President
National Association of State
  Boards of Education

Dr. Anna J. Harrison
Professor Emeritus, Chemistry
  Mount Holyoke College; and
  President, American Association
  for the Advancement of Science

Dr. M. Joan Parent
President, National School Boards
   Association

Dr. Frank Press
President
National Academy of Sciences

Chief Staffperson

Roy H. Forbes
Associate Executive Director
Education Commission of the States

Report Preparation

Ervin S. Duggan Associates

Board of Trustees of the Twentieth Century Fund

Morris B. Abram
Peter A.A. Berle, Chairman
Jonathan B. Bingham
Jose A. Cabranes
Hodding Carter III
Brewster C. Denny
Daniel J. Evans
Charles V. Hamilton
Patricia Roberts Harris
August Heckscher
Matina S. Horner

James A. Leach
Georges-Henri Martin
P. Michael Pitfield
Richard Ravitch
William D. Ruckelshaus
Arthur M. Schlesinger, Jr.
Harvey I. Sloane, M.D.
James Tobin
David B. Truman
Shirley Williams, M.P.
M.J. Rossant, Director

Task Force Members (The Twentieth Century Fund)

Robert Wood, Chairman
Henry R. Luce Professor of
   Democratic Institutions and Social
   Order
Wesleyan University formerly
   Director of Urban Studies
University of Massachusetts

Brewster C. Denny
Professor of Public Affairs
formerly Dean, Graduate School of
   Public Affairs
University of Washington

Chester E. Finn, Jr.
Codirector and Professor of
   Education and Public Policy
Center on Education Policy
Institute for Public Policy Studies
Vanderbilt University

Patricia Albjerg Graham
Dean and Charles Warren Professor
   of the History of Educattion
Graduate School of Education
Harvard University

Charles V. Hamilton
Wallace S. Sayre Professor of
  Government
Department of Political Science
Columbia University

Carlos R. Hortas
Chairman
Department of Romance Languages
Hunter College

Diane Ravitch
Adjunct Associate Professor
Teachers College
Columbia University

Wilson Riles
Wilson Riles & Associates,
  Sacramento
Formerly Superintendent of Public
  Instruction and Director of
  Education
State Department of Education,
  Sacramento

Donald M. Steward
President
Spelman College
Atlanta

Robert E. Wentz
Superintendent
Clark County School District
Las Vegas

Rosalyn Yalow
Chairman
Department of Clinical Science
Montefiore Medical Center
New York

Rapporteur: Paul E. Peterson
Professor of Political Science and
  Education
Department of Political Science
University of Chicago

Members of the National Science Board Commission on Precollege Education in Mathematics, Science and Technology

William T. Coleman, Jr. Co-Chair
Senior Partner
O'Melveny and Meyers
Washington, D.C., New York, N.Y.
Los Angeles, California, and Paris,
  France; former U.S. Secretary of
  Transportation in the Ford
  Administration

Cecily Cannan Selby, Co-Chair
New York, N.Y.; former Dean of
  Academic Affairs and Chair
Board of Advisors
North Carolina School of Science and
  Mathematics

Lew Allen, Jr.
Director
Jet Propulsion Laboratory and Vice
  President
California Institute of Technology
former Chief of Staff
U.S. Air Force

Victoria Begin
Associate Commissioner of
  Education for the State of Texas

George Burnet, Jr.
Chairman
Nuclear Engineering Department
Iowa State University; former
  President
American Society for Engineering
  Education

William H. Cosby, Jr.
Entertainer/Educator

Daniel J. Evans
President
The Evergreen State College
former Governor of the State of
  Washington

Patricia Albjerg Graham
Dean Graduate School of Education
Harvard University

Robert E. Larson
Chief Executive Officer
Optimization Technology, Inc.
former President, Institute of
  Electrical and Electronics
  Engineers

Gerald D. Laubach
President
Pfizer Inc.

Katherine P. Layton
Teacher
Mathematics Department
Beverly Hills High School

Ruth B. Love
General Superintendent
The Chicago Board of Education

Arturo Madrid II
Professor
Department of Spanish and
  Portuguese
University of Minnesota
former Director, Fund for the
  Improvement of Postsecondary
  Education
U.S. Department of Education

Frederick Mosteller
Chairman
Department of Health Policy and
  Management
School of Public Health
Harvard University

M. Joan Parent
President
National School Boards Association

Robert W. Parry
Distinguished Professor of
  Chemistry
University of Utah; former President
American Chemical Society

Benjamin F. Payton
President
Tuskegee Institute

Joseph E. Rowe
Executive Vice President
Research and Defense Systems,
  Gould, Inc.
former Provost for Science and
  Engineering
Case Western Reserve University

Herbert A. Simon
Richard King Mellon University
Professor of Computer Science and
  Psychology
Department of Psychology
Carnegie-Mellon University
Nobel Laureate in Economics

John B. Slaughter
Chancellor
University of Maryland
College Park
former Director, National Science
  Foundation

A Study of High Schools

Theodore R. Sizer, Chairman   Arthur G. Powell
                                     Executive Director

Co-sponsored by the National Association of Secondary School Principals and the Commission on Educational Issues of the National Association of Independent Schools.

Appendix C: Commissioned Papers Accompanying A Nation at Risk

Author(s)

Clifford Adelman
  National Institute of Education
  Washington, D.C.

'A Study of High School Transcripts 1964–1981' ED 228 244

Joseph Adelson
  University of Michigan, Ann
  Arbor

'Twenty-Five Years of American Education: An Interpretation' ED 227 108

Catherine P. Ailes
Francis W. Rushing
  SRI International, Arlington, VA

'A Summary Report on the Educational Systems of the United States and the Soviet Union: Comparative Analysis' ED 227 106

Alexander W. Astin
  University of California,
  Los Angeles

'Excellence and Equity in American Education' ED 227 098

Alexander W. Astin
  University of California,
  Los Angeles

'The American Freshman, 1966–1981: Some Implications for Educational Policy and Practice' ED 227 070

Herman Blake
  University of California, Santa
  Cruz

'Demographic Change and Curriculum: New Students in Higher Education' ED 225 994

Richard I. Brod
  The Modern Language
  Association, New York, New
  York
Nicholas Farnham
  The International Council on the
  Future of the University, New
  York, New York

'University Entrance Examinations and Performance Expectations' ED 227 102

William V. Mayer
  Biological Sciences Curriculum
  Study Boulder, Colorado
Robert A. McCaughey
  Bernard College, New York, New
  York

Barbara B. Burn   'An Analytic Comparison of
Christopher H. Hurn   Educational Systems' ED 225 991
  University of Massachusetts,
  Amherst

Philip Cusick   'Secondary Public Schools in
  Michigan State University, East   America' ED 227 105
  Lansing

Paul DeHart Hurd   'An Overview of Science Education
  Stanford University, CA   in the United States and Selected
                                       Foreign Countries' ED 227 076

Walter Doyle   'Academic Work' ED 227 097
  University of Texas at Austin

Kenneth Duckworth   'Some Ideas About Student
  University of Oregon, Eugene   Cognition, Motivation and Work'
                                       (A Critique of the Symposium on
                                       The Student's Role in Learning)
                                       ED 228 240

Max A. Eckstein   'A Comparative Review of
  Queens College/City of New York   Curriculum: Mathematics and
  Flushing   International Studies in the
Susanne Shafer   Secondary Schools of Five
  Arizona State University, Tempe   Countries' ED 227 068
Kenneth Travers
  University of Illinois,
  Champaign–Urbana

Eleanor Farrar   'Effective Schools Programs in High
  The Huron Institute, Cambridge,   Schools: Implications for Policy,
  Massachusetts   Practice and Research' ED 228 243
Matthew B. Miles
  Center for Policy Research, New
  York, New York
Barbara Neufeld
  The Huron Institute, Cambridge,
  Massachusetts

Zelda Gamson   'A Little Light on the Subject:
  University of Michigan, Ann   Keeping General and Liberal
  Arbor   Education Alive' ED 225 993

William E. Gardner
  University of Minnesota,
  Minneapolis
John R. Palmer
  University of Wisconsin, Madison
	'Certification and Accreditation:
	  Background, Issue Analysis, and
	  Recommendations' ED 226 003

Thomas L. Good
  University of Missouri-Columbia
	'What Is Learned in Schools:
	  Responding to School Demands,
	  Grades K-6' ED 227 100

Thomas L. Good and
Gail M. Hinkel
  University of Missouri-Columbia
	'Schooling in America: Some
	  Descriptive and Explanatory
	  Statements' ED 228 246

Donald B. Holsinger
  State University of New York,
  Albany
	'Time, Content and Expectations as
	  Predictors of School Achievement
	  in the U.S.A. and Other
	  Developed Countries: A Review of
	  IEA Evidence' ED 227 077

Kenneth R. Howey
  University of Minnesota,
  Minneapolis
	'Charting Directions for Pre-Service
	  Teacher Education' ED 226 004

Torsten Husén
  University of Stockholm, Sweden
	'A Cross-National Perspective on
	  Assessing the Quality of Learning'
	  ED 225 992

Nancy Karweit
  Johns Hopkins University
  Baltimore, MD
	'Time on Task: A Research Review'
	  ED 228 236

Howard London
  Bridgewater State College
  Massachusetts
	'Academic Standards in the American
	  Community College: Trends and
	  Controversies' ED 227 071

Martin L. Maehr
  University of Illinois,
  Champaign-Urbana
	'Motivational Factors in School
	  Achievement' ED 227 106

Matthew B. Miles
  Center for Policy Research, New
  York, New York
Eleanor Farrar and
Barbara Neufeld
  The Huron Institute, Cambridge,
  Massachusetts
	'The Extent of Adoption of Effective
	  Schools Programs' ED 228 242

Barbara Neufeld and
Eleanor Farrar
  The Huron Institute, Cambridge,
  Massachusetts
	'A Review of Effective Schools
	  Research: The Message for
	  Secondary Schools' ED 228 241

Matthew B. Miles
  Center for Policy Research, New
  York, New York

William Neumann
  Syracuse University, New York

'College Press and Student Fit' ED
227 112

C. Robert Pace
  University of California,
  Los Angeles

'Achievement and Quality of Student
Effort' ED 227 101

Harvey L. Prokop
  San Diego Unified School District,
  CA

'Intelligence, Motivation and the
Quantity and Quality of Academic
Work and Their Impacts on the
Learning of Students: A
Practitioner's Reaction' (A Critique
of the Symposium on *The Student's
Role in Learning*) ED 227 103

Lauren B. Resnick
  University of Pittsburgh, PA

'Standards, Curriculum, and
Performance: An Historical and
Comparative Perspective'
ED 227 104

Daniel P. Resnick
  Carnegie-Mellon University
  Pittsburgh, PA

Frederick Rudolph
  Williams College
  Williamstown, MA

'Educational Excellence — The
Secondary School — College and
Other Matters: An Historical
Assessment' ED 225 995

Clifford Sjogren
  University of Michigan, Ann
  Arbor

'College Admissions and the
Transition to Postsecondary
Education: Standards and Practices'
ED 227 094

Richard E. Snow
  Stanford University, CA

'Intelligence, Motivation and
Academic Work' (A Critique of the
Symposium on *The Student's Role
in Learning*) ED 227 107

Robert J. Sternberg
Richard Wagner
  Yale University, New Haven,
  Connecticut

'Understanding Intelligence: What's
in It for Educators?' ED 227 110

Deborah Stipek
  University of California,
  Los Angeles

'Motivating Students to Learn: A
Lifelong Perspective' ED 227 111

Judith Torney-Purta
  University of Maryland, College
  Park
John Schwille
  Michigan State University, East
  Lansing

'The Values Learned in School:
  Policy and Practice in
  Industrialized Countries'
  ED 227 072

Beatrice Ward
John R. Mergendoller
Alexis L. Mitman
  Far West Laboratory for
  Educational Research and
  Development, San Francisco, CA

'The Years Between Elementary
  School and High School: What
  Schooling Experiences Do
  Students Have?' ED 228 239

Jonathan Warran
  Educational Testing Service
  Berkeley, CA

'The Faculty Role in Educational
  Excellence' ED 227 069

Dean K. Whitla
  Harvard University Cambridge,
  Massachusetts

'Value Added and Other Related
  Matters' ED 228 245

Sam J. Yarger
  Syracuse University, New York

'Inservice Education' ED 227 075

Herbert Zimiles
  Bank Street College of Education
  New York, New York

'The Changing American Child: The
  Perspective of Educators'
  ED 227 099

Bibliography

ADLER, M.J. (1982), *The Paideia Proposal: An Educational Manifesto*, New York: MacMillan.

ADVISORY PANEL ON FINANCING ELEMENTARY AND SECONDARY EDUCATION, (1982), *Toward More Local Control: Financial Reform for Public Education*, Washington, DC: U.S. Government Printing Office, 31 December.

AFDC CUTS HURT, (1984), *ISR Newsletter*, University of Michigan, Spring/Summer, p. 3.

ALBRECHT, J.E. (1984), 'A nation at risk: Another view', *Phi Delta Kappan*, 65(10), June, pp. 684–5.

ALMY, M. (1975), *Ways of Studying Children*, New York: Teachers College Press.

AMERICAN ASSEMBLY, (1960), *Goals for Americans: The Report of the President's Commission on National Goals*, Englewood Cliffs, NJ: Prentice-Hall-Spectrum Book.

ANALYZING LITERATURE 'DIFFICULT' FOR MANY, (1981), *National Assessment of Educational Progress Newsletter*, XIV(3), Fall, pp. 1, 2, 4.

APPLE, M.W. (1983), Curriculum in the year 2000: Tensions and possibilities, *Phi Delta Kappan*, 64(5), January, pp. 321–6.

ARLIN, P.K. (1975), 'Cognitive development in adulthood: A fifth stage', *Developmental Psychology*, 11(5), pp. 602–6.

BAKALIS, M.J. (1983), 'Power and purpose in American education', *Phi Delta Kappan*, 65(1), September, pp. 7–13.

BAKER, E.L. (1984), 'Can educational research inform educational practice? Yes!', *Phi Delta Kappan*, 65(7), March, pp. 453–5.

BAILEY, A.Y. (1983), 'The educational equality project: Focus on results', *Phi Delta Kappan*, 65(1), September, pp. 22–5.

BELL, H. (1983), *Goals and Performance Priorities of the U.S. Department of Education for Fiscal year 1984*, Washington, DC: United States Department of Education, 28 November, 17 pp. (photocopy).

BELL, T.H. (1984), 'American education at a crossroads', *Phi Delta Kappan*, 65(8), April, pp. 531–4.

BERLAK, A. and BERLAK, H. (1983), 'Toward a non-hierarchical approach to school inquiry and leadership', *Curriculum Inquiry*, 13(3), February, pp. 267–94.

BERNSTEIN, H. (1982), 'Metacognition or taking study skills out of the closet', *Basic Education*, 27(4), December, pp. 12–14.

BEST, J.H. (1984), Reforming America's schools: The high risks of failure, *Teachers College Record*, 86(2), Winter, pp. 265–74.

BEYER, B.K. (1983), 'Common sense about teaching thinking skills', *Educational Leadership*, 41(3), November, pp. 44–9.

BEYER, B.K. (1984a), 'Improving thinking skills — defining the problem', *Phi Delta Kappan*, 65(7), March, pp. 486–90.

BEYER, B.K. (1984b), 'Improving thinking skills — practical approaches', *Phi Delta kappan*, 65(8), April, pp. 556–60.

BEYER, L.E. (1985), 'Educational reform: The political roots of national risk', *Curriculum Inquiry*, 15(1), Spring, pp. 37–56.

BIVENS, T. (1984), 'Helping advertising money talk for business in foreign markets', *Philadelphia Inquirer*, 9 July, p. 8C.

BLOCH, M. (1964), *The Historian's Craft*, New York: Vintage Books.

BLOOM, B.S. (1984), 'The 2 sigma problem: The search for methods of group instruction as effective as one-to-one tutoring', *Educational Researcher*, 13(6), June/July, pp. 4–16.

BLUESTONE, B. *et al.* (1985), 'Do we need an industrial policy?' *Harper's Magazine*, 270(1617), February, pp. 35–44.

BOFFEY, P.M. (1984), 'Industry takes dominant science role', *New York Times*, 17 July, pp. C1, C9.

BOK, D. (1984), 'Needed: A new way to train doctors', *Harvard Magazine*, 86(5), May/June, pp. 32–43 and 70–1.

BOYER, E.L. (1983), *High School: A Report on Secondary Education in America*, New York: Harper & Row.

BOYER, E.L. (1984), Reflections on the great debate of '83', *Phi Delta Kappan*, 65(8), April, pp. 525–30.

BRECKENRIDGE, P. (1984), 'Florida school chief calls for slowdown of state reform efforts', *Education Week*, Vol. III(37 and 38), 6 June, pp. 7 and 34.

BRIDGMAN, A. (1984a), 'International math assessment finds U.S. students "average"', *Education Week*, III(34), 16 May, p. 1, 17.

BRIDGMAN, A. (1984b), 'Oregon board to vote on action plan for excellence', *Education Week*, III(37 & 38), 6 June, p. 6.

BRIDGMAN, A. (1985), 'States launching barrage of initiatives, survey finds', *Education Week*, IV(20), 6 February, pp. 1 and 31.

BROAD, W.J. (1984), 'Does genius or technology rule science?' *New York Times*, 7 August, pp. C1, C10.

BROUDY, H.S. (1982), What knowledge is of most worth? *Educational Leadership*, 39(8), May, pp. 574–8.

BROWN, B.F. (1973), *The Reform of Secondary Education: A Report to the Public and the Profession*, The National Commission on the Reform of Secondary Education, New York: McGraw-Hill.

BROWN, J.S. (1983), 'Process versus product: A perspective on tools for communal and informal electronic learning', reprinted from *Report From the Learning Lab: Education in the Electronic Age*, Educational Broadcasting Corporation, (photocopy).

BROWN, J.S. (1984), *Idea Amplifiers — New Kinds of Electronic Learning Environ-*

ments, reprinted from Claremont Reading Conference, Claremont Graduate School of Education, Claremont, CA, March, (photocopy).

BRUNER, J.S. (1960), *The Process of Education*, New York: Vintage Books.

BRUNER, J.S. (1966), *Toward a Theory of Instruction*, Cambridge, MA: The Belknap Press.

BUREAU OF THE CENSUS, (1984), *Current Population Reports, Nursery School and Kindergarten Enrollment*, Washington, DC: U.S. Department of Commerce, Series P-20.

BUTTS, R.F. (1979), 'The revival of civic learning', *Social Education*, 43(5), May, pp. 359–64.

CALIFORNIA STUDY ASSESSES FACTORS IN SCHOOL EFFECTIVENESS, (1984), *Education Week*, III(29), 11 April, p. 3.

CARNOY, M. (1983), 'Education, democracy, and social conflict', *Harvard Education Review*, 53(4), November, pp. 398–402.

CHILDREN FALLING INTO POVERTY NEED SPECIAL HELP, CDF REPORTS, (1984), *Report on Education Research*, 16(2), 18 January, p. 5.

CLABAUGH, G.K., FEDEN, P.D. and VOGEL, R. (1984), 'Revolutionizing teacher education: Training developmentally oriented teachers', *Phi Delta Kappan*, 65(4), May, pp. 615–6.

CLARK, B.R. (1985), 'The high school and the university: What went wrong in America, Part 1', *Phi Delta Kappan*, 66(6), February, pp. 391–7.

CLEMENT, J.P. (1983), '"A Nation at Risk": At best, a C+', *Independent School*, 43(1), October, pp. 19–22.

COHEN, D.K. and NEUFELD, B. (1981), 'The failure of high schools and the progress of education', *Daedalus*, 110(3), Summer, pp. 69–89.

COHEN, S. (1984), 'San Francisco: A city with a long-standing love for the eccentric', *Philadelphia Inquirer*, 9 July, p. 4A.

COHN, M.M. and DISTEFANO, A. (1984), 'The recommendations of the National Commission on Excellence in Education: A case study of their value', *Issues in Education*, II(3), Winter, pp. 204–220.

COLEMAN, J.S. (1985), International comparisons of cognitive achievement, *Phi Delta Kappan*, 66(6), February, pp. 403–6.

THE COLLEGE BOARD, (1983), *Academic Preparation for College: What Students Need to Know and Be Able to Do*, New York: The College Board.

COMMAGER, H.S. (1984), Tocqueville's mistake, *Harper's Magazine*, 269(1611), August, pp. 70–4.

THE COMMITTEE OF TEN, (1893), *Report of the Committee of Ten on Secondary School Studies*, Washington, DC: United States Bureau of Education.

CONANT, J.B. (1959), *The American High School Today*, New York: McGraw-Hill.

CONNELL, C. (1985), 'Schools accused of ignoring special needs', *Philadelphia Inquirer*, 29 January, pp. 1A, 4A.

COOKE, R. (1984), 'Goode task force: Hispanics hold few city jobs, and half live in poverty', *Philadelphia Inquirer*, 8 August, p. 3B.

CORDES, C. (1984), 'Reuven Feuerstein makes every child count', *APA Monitor*, 15(5), May, pp. 8 and 20.

COSTA, A.L. (1981), 'Teaching for intelligent behavior', *Educational Leadership*, 39(1), October, pp. 29–32.

COSTA, A.L. (1984), 'Mediating the metacognitive', *Educational Leadership*, 42(3), November, pp. 57–62.

CRAIN, R.L. (1984), *The Quality of American High School Graduates: What Personnel Officers Say and Do About It*, Baltimore, MD: Center for Social Organization of Schools, Report no. 354, May.

CRANDALL, D.P. (1984), *Building an Infrastructure for Innovation and Improvement: Short-term and Long-term Strategies*, Andover, MA: the Network, April.

CREMIN, L.A. (1977), *Traditions of American Education*, New York: Basic Books.

CUBAN, L. (1979), 'Determinants of curriculum change and stability, 1870–1970', in SCHAFFARZICK J. and SYKES G., (Eds), *Value Conflicts and Curriculum Issues*, Berkeley, CA: McCutchan, pp. 139–90.

CUBAN, L. (1982), Persistent instruction: The high school classroom, 1900–1980', *Phi Delta Kappan*, 64(2), October, pp. 113–8.

CUBAN, L. (1983), 'Corporate involvement in public schools: A practitioner-academic's perspective', *Teachers College Record*, 85(2), Winter, pp. 183–95.

CUBAN, L. (1984), 'Transforming the frog into a prince: Effective schools research, policy, and practice at the district level', *Harvard Educational Review*, 54(2), May, pp. 129–51.

DARLING-HAMMOND, L. (1984a), *Beyond the Commission Reports: The Coming Crisis in Teaching*, Santa Monica, CA: Rand Corporation.

DARLING-HAMMOND, L. (1984b), 'Mad-hatter tests of good teaching', *The New York Times*, section 12, 8 January, p. 57.

DEWEY, J. (1938), *Experience and Education*, London: Collier-Macmillan.

DEWEY, J. (1971), *The Child and the Curriculum and The School and Society*, Chicago: The University of Chicago Press.

DIANDA, M. (1984), *The Superintendent's Can-do Guide to School Improvement*, Washington, DC: Council for Educational Development and Research.

DOUGLASS, H.R. (1964), *The High School Curriculum*, New York: The Ronald Press.

DOYLE, D.P. and COOPER, B.S. (1983), 'Is excellence possible in urban public schools?' *American Education*, 19(9), November, pp. 16–26.

DOYLE, W. (1982), *Academic Work*, Washington, DC: paper prepared for the National Commission on Excellence in Education, (photocopy).

DREYFUS, H.L. and DREYFUS, S.E. (1984), 'Putting computers in their proper place: Analysis versus intuition in the classroom', *Teachers College Record*, 85(4), Summer, pp. 578–601.

DURÁN, R.P. (1983), *Hispanics' Education and Background: Predictors of College Achievement*, New York: College Entrance Examination Board.

EDELFELT, R.A. (1984), *Policy Questions Prompted by Seven Recent Reports on Education*, Washington, DC: Edelfelt Johnson, June.

EDMONDS, R. (1980), Schools count: New York City's school improvement project. *Harvard Graduate School of Education Association Bulletin*, XXV(1), Fall, pp. 33–5.

EDSON, C.H. (1983), 'Risking the Nation: Historical dimensions on survival and educational reform', *Issues in Education: Educational Dilemmas of the*

'80's, 1(2+3), Washington, DC: American Educational Research Association.

EDUCATION SCHOOLS IN MIDST OF REFORM, AACTE SURVEY SAYS, (1984), *Report on Education Research*, 16(16), 1 August, p. 4.

EISNER, E.W. (Ed.) (1971), *Confronting Curriculum Reform*, Boston: Little, Brown.

EISNER, E.W. (1982), *Cognition and Curriculum: A Basis for Deciding What to Teach*, New York: Longman.

EISNER, E.W. (1983), 'The kind of schools we need', *Educational Leadership*, 41(2), October, pp. 48–55.

EISNER, E.W. (1984), 'Can educational research inform educational practice?', *Phil Delta Kappan*, 65(7), March, pp. 447–52.

ETZIONI, A. (1982), 'The role of self-discipline', *Phi Delta Kappan*, 64(3), November, pp. 184–9.

FARRAR, E., NEUFELD, B. and MILES, M.B. (1984), 'Effective schools programs in high schools: Social promotion or movement by merit?' *Phi Delta Kappan*, 65(10), June, pp. 701–6.

FEISTRITZER, C.E. (1984), *The Making of a Teacher: A Report on Teacher Education and Certification*, Washington, DC: National Center for Educational Information.

FELDMAN, B.S. (1984), Great expectatious of yesteryear's teacher, *New York Times*, 6 May, p. 22E.

FENSTERMACHER, G.D. (1984), The pre-service improvement project in retrospect, *Journal of Teacher Education, XXXV*(4), July/August, pp. 28–30.

FEUERSTEIN, R. (1980), *Instrumental Enrichment*, Baltimore, MD: University Park Press.

FEUERSTEIN, R., MILLER, R., HOFFMAN, M.B., RAND, Y., MINTZKER, Y. and JENSEN, M.R. (1981), 'Cognitive modifiability in adolescence: Cognitive structure and the effects of intervention', *Journal of Special Education*, 15(2), pp. 269–87.

FINKELSTEIN, B. (1984), 'Education and the retreat from democracy in the United States, 1979–198?', *Teachers College Record*, 86(2), Winter, pp. 275–82.

FINN, C.E., JR. (1984a), 'Toward strategic independence: Nine commandments for enhancing school effectiveness', *Phi Delta Kappan*, 65(8), April, pp. 518–24.

FINN, C.E., JR. (1984b), 'The excellence backlash: Sources of resistance to educational reform', *The American Spectator*, 17(9), September, pp. 10–16.

FINN, C.E., JR. (1985), 'Teacher unions and school quality: potential allies or inevitable foes?' *Phi Delta Kappan*, 66(5), January, pp. 331–8.

FIVE HUNDRED THOUSAND (500,000) MORE TEACHERS TO BE NEEDED BY 1995, (1984), *Report on Education Research*, 16(2), 18 January, p. 4.

FISKE, E.B. (1984a), 'New look at effective schools', *The New York Times*, 15 April, pp. 1, 35–6 and 55–6.

FISKE, E.B. (1984b), 'U.S. pupils lag from grade 1, study finds', *New York Times*, 17 June, pp. 1 and 30.

FLORIO, D.H. (1983), 'Curing America's quick-fix mentality: A role for federally supported educational research', *Phi Delta Kappan*, 64(6), February, pp. 411–5.

FORD FOUNDATION, (1984), *City High Schools: A Recognition of Progress*, New York: Ford Foundation.

FORD TO NEARLY DOUBLE PROGRAM SUPPORT FOR HISPANICS, (1984), *Report on Education Research*, 16(18), 29 August, p. 4.

FUTRELL, M.H. (1985), 'Chester Finn and quality education', *Phi Delta Kappan*, 66(5), January, pp. 339–40.

GADD, C.J. and KRAMER, S.N. (1966), *Ur Excavation Texts*, Plate CCLXIV (no. 341), London and Philadelphia: Joint Expedition of the British Museum and the University Museum, University of Pennsylvania.

GARDNER, H. (1983), *Frames of Mind: The Theory of Multiple Intelligences*, New York: Basic Books.

GARDNER, J.W. (1961), *Excellence: Can We Be Equal and Excellent Too?* New York: Harper and Row.

GIBBONEY, R.A. (1983), 'Learning: A process approach from Francis Parker', *Phi Delta Kappan*, 65(1), September, pp. 55–6.

GINSBERG, R. and WIMPELBERG, R.K. (1985), 'The national reform reports', *Educational and Urban Society*, 17(2), February.

GIROUX, H.A. (1984), 'Public philosophy and the crisis in education', *Harvard Educational Review*, 54(2), May, pp. 186–94.

GLAZER, N. (1984), 'The problem with competence', *American Journal of Education*, 92(3), May, pp. 306–13.

GOLDBERG, M. and HARVEY, J. (1983), 'A Nation at Risk: The report of the National Commission on Excellence in Education', *Phi Delta Kappan*, 65(1), September, pp. 14–18.

GOLDMAN, L. (1984), 'Matters of fact and the facts of the matter', *The High School Journal*, 68(1), October/November, pp. 1–5.

GOODLAD, J.I. (1983), 'Access to knowledge', *Teachers College Record*, 84(4), Summer, pp. 787–800.

GOODLAD, J.I. (1984), *A Place called School: Prospects for the Future*. New York: McGraw-Hill.

GRAHAM, P.A. (1983), 'The Twentieth Century Fund task force report on federal elementary and secondary education policy', *Phi Delta Kappan*, 65(1), September, pp. 19–21.

GRAHAM, P.A. (1984), 'Schools: Cacophony about practice, silence about purpose', *Daedalus*, 113(4), Fall, pp. 29–57.

GRAUBARD, S.R. (1983), 'Confronting the obvious: Social class and its devastating effects on American schooling', *Daedalus*, 112(3), Summer, pp. 191–209.

GRAUBARD, S.R. (1984), Zeal, cunning, candor, and persistence — to what educational ends? *Daedalus*, 113(4), Fall, pp. 75–106.

HAHN, R.O. and BIDNA, D.E. (1965), *Secondary Education: Origins and Directions*, New York: Macmillan.

HAMBURG, D.A. (1983), *The Context for Carnegie Corporation's New Grant Programs*, New York: Carnegie Corporation of New York.

HARPER'S INDEX (1984), *Harper's Magazine*, 268(1608), May, p. 9.

HARVEY, G. (1984), *Recent Reports Concerning Education or the Road to*

Nirvana: You Can't Get There From Here, Andover, MA: The Network, April.

HASKINS, W.J. (1983), 'The black community and teenage pregnancy', *Education Week*, II(32), 4 May, p. 18.

HECHINGER, F.M. (1984), 'German math scores cause alarm in Britain', *New York Times*, 13 March.

HERTLING, J. (1985), 'Reagan panel warns high dropout rate threatens business', *Education Week*, IV(25), 13 March, p. 1, 14.

HOFSTADTER, R. (1966), *Anti-intellectualism in American Life*, New York: Vintage Books.

HOLTON, G. (1984), 'A Nation at Risk revisited', *Daedalus*, 113(4), Fall, pp. 1–27.

HONIG, B. (1984), 'Setting the course for school reform', *Education Week*, III(30), 18 April, pp. 19, 24.

HOWARD, M. (1985), 'The bewildered American raj: Reflections on a democracy's foreign policy', *Harper's Magazine*, 270 (1618), March, pp. 55–60.

HOWE, H. II. (1983), 'Education moves to center stage: An overview of recent studies', *Phi Delta Kappan*, 65(3), November, pp. 167–72.

HOWE, H. II. (1984), 'More-of-the same reform will not achieve both excellence and equity', *Education Week*, III(35), 23 May, pp. 19 and 24.

HUNT, J.B., JR. (1984), 'Education for economic growth: A critical investment', *Phi Delta Kappan*, 65(8), April, pp. 538–41.

HURN, C. (1983), 'The problem with comparisons', *Educational Leadership*, 41(2), October, pp. 7–12.

HUSÉN, T. (1983), 'Are standards in U.S. schools really lagging behind those in other countries?', *Phi Delta Kappan*, 64(8), March, pp. 455–61.

HUSÉN, T. (1985), 'The school in the achievement-oriented society: crisis and reform', *Phi Delta Kappan*, 66(6), February, pp. 398–402.

IRVING, K.J. (1984), 'Cross-cultural awareness and the English-as-a-second language classroom', *Theory Into Practice*, XXIII(2), Spring, pp. 138–43.

IRWIN, J. (1984), 'Study: U.S. pupils lack family help', *Philadelphia Inquirer*, 18 June, p. 5A.

JACOBSON, W.J. and DORAN, R.L. (1985), 'The second international science study: U.S. results', *Phi Delta Kappan*, 66(6), February, pp. 414–7.

JAMES, T. and TYACK, D. (1983), 'Learning from past efforts to reform the high school', *Phi Delta Kappan*, 64(5), February, pp. 400–6.

JOHNSON, D.W., JOHNSON, R.T., HOLUBEC, E.J. and ROY, P. (1984), *Circles of Learning*, Alexandria, VA: Association for Supervision and Curriculum Development.

JOHNSON, S.M. (1984), 'Merit pay for teachers: A poor prescription for reform', *Harvard Educational Review*, 54(2), May, pp. 175–85.

JOYCE, B. and CLIFT, R. (1984), 'The phoenix agenda: Essential reform in teacher education', *Educational Researcher*, 13(4), April, pp. 5–19.

JUSTIZ, M.J. (1984), 'Improving teacher education through research', *Journal of Teacher Education*, XXXV(4), July/August, p. 2.

KAESTLE, C.F. (1978), 'Social reform and the urban school: An essay review', in WARREN, D.R. (Ed.), *History, Education, and Public Policy*, Berkeley, CA: McCutchan, pp. 127–47.

KAESTLE, C.F. (1985), 'Education reform and the swinging pendulum', *Phi Delta Kappan*, 66(6), February, pp. 422–3.

KAMII, C. (1984), 'Autonomy: The aim of education envisioned by Piaget', *Phi Delta Kappan*, 65(6), February, pp. 410–5.

KATZ, M.B. (1975), *Class Bureaucracy and Schools: The Illusion of Educational Change in America*, New York: Praeger.

KAUFMAN, M. (1984), 'Refugees rise to the top of the class', *Philadelphia Inquirer*, 24 June, pp. 1B and 10B.

KEELY, C.B. (1982), 'Illegal migration', *Scientific American*, 246(3), March, pp. 41–8.

KENTUCKY RULES THAT ENGLISH IS SOLE OFFICIAL LANGUAGE, (1984), *Philadelphia Inquirer*, 10 July, p. 2A.

KIMELMAN, D. (1984), 'Communist party leaders favor wide changes in Soviet education', *Philadelphia Inquirer*, 11 April.

KLEIN, E.L. (Ed.) (1985), *Children and Computers*, San Francisco: Jossey Bass.

KLUENDER, M.M. (1984), 'Teacher education programs in the 1980s: Some selected characteristics', *Journal of Teacher Education*, XXXV(4), July/ August, pp. 33–5.

LANIER, J.E. (1984), 'The preservice teacher education improvement project: A critical review', *Journal of Teacher Education*, XXXV(4), July/August, pp. 24–7.

LAPHAM, L.H. (1984), 'A society at war with its children', *Philadelphia Inquirer*, 14 August, p. 11A.

LAPOINTE, A.E. (1984), 'The good news about American education', *Phi Delta Kappan*, 65(10), June, pp. 663–7.

LARSON, R.L. (1984), 'School improvement through a cultural lens', *Teachers College Record*, 85(4), Summer, pp. 670–5.

LAZERSON, M. (1985), 'Remembering yesterday's lessons as we improve today's schools', *Education Week*, IV(18), 23 January, p. 32.

LAZERSON, M., McLAUGHLIN, J.B. and McPHERSON, B. (1984), 'New curriculum, old issues', *Teachers College Record*, 86(2), Winter, pp. 299–319.

LEONARD, G. (1984), 'The great school reform hoax', *Esquire*, 101(4), April, pp. 47–56.

LEVIN, H.M. and RUMBERGER, R.W. (1983), 'Secondary education in an age of high technology', *NASSP Bulletin*, 67(467), December, pp. 49–55.

LIEBERMAN, A. (1984), 'The curriculum reform debate: Some critical issues', *Teachers College Record*, 85(4), Summer, pp. 663–670.

LIEBERMAN, M. (1984), 'Here's why the key recommendations of the excellence commission never will become reality', *The American School Board Journal*, 171(2), February, pp. 32–3.

LIEBERMAN, M. (1985), 'Teacher unions and educational quality: Folklore by Finn', *Phi Delta Kappan*, 66(5), January, pp. 341–3.

LIKING KIDS IS ONE SECRET TO GOOD SCHOOLS, (1984), *The American School Board Journal*, 171(7), July, pp. 13–14.

LINN, M.C. (1982), *The Importance of Cognitive Psychology in Curriculum Development and Teacher Education*. Washington, DC: National Commission on Excellence in Education, 28 pp., (photocopy).

LOEB, V. (1984a), 'Some fear more courses mean more dropouts', *Philadelphia*

Inquirer, 9 May, pp. 1B and 4B.

LOEB, V. (1984b), 'School board delays stricter promotions policy', *Philadelphia Inquirer*, 19 July, p. 1B.

LOEB, V. (1984c), 'Competency tests called burden for schools', *Philadelphia Inquirer*, 8 August, p. 1B, 2B.

LOHR, S. (1984), 'The Japanese challenge', *The New York Times Magazine*, pp. 18–23, 37, 39 and 41.

LOUCKS-HORSLEY, S. and COX, P.L. (1984), *Its all in the doing: What recent research says about implementation*, (paper presented at AERA), Andover, MA: The Network. (photocopy), April.

MACHADO, L.A. (1980), *The Right to be Intelligent*, New York: Pergamon.

MARQUEZ, M. (1984), 'More people under 35 found living together — or staying at home', *Philadelphia Inquirer*, 19 July, p. 10A.

MARTIN, D. (1984), 'Will the dawn of cooperative employment bank your workers' fire?', *The American School Board Journal*, 171(7), July, pp. 18–23.

McCARTY, G. (1984), 'Boyer urges recognition of the "dignity of teaching"', *Education Week*, III(32), 2 May, p. 11.

McCORMICK, T.E. (1984), 'Multiculturalism: Some principles and issues', *Theory Into Practice*, XXIII(2), Spring, pp. 93–7.

McNETT, I. (1984), *Charting a Course: A Guide to the Excellence Movement in Education*, Washington, DC: Council for Basic Education.

MILLS, J. (1984), 'U.S. Hispanic population is reported at 16 million', *Philadelphia Inquirer*, 16 April, p. 9A.

MITCHELL, D.E. and ENCARNATION, D.J. (1984), 'Alternative state policy mechanisms for influencing school performance', *Educational Researcher*, 13(5), May, pp. 4–11.

MULLIS, I.V.S. (1984), *What do NAEP Results tell us about Students' Higher Order Thinking Abilities*, Racine, WI: Association for Supervision and Curriculum Development Conference at Wingspread, May 21 pp. (photocopy).

NATIONAL ACADEMY OF SCIENCES (Committee on Science, Engineering and Public Policy), (1984), *High Schools and the Changing Workplace*, Washington, DC: National Academy Press.

NATIONAL COALITION OF ADVOCATES FOR STUDENTS, (1985), *Barriers to Excellence: Our Children at Risk*. Boston, MA: National Coalition of Advocates for Students, January.

NATIONAL COMMISSION ON EXCELLENCE IN EDUCATION, (1983a), *A Nation at Risk: The Imperative for Educational Reform*. Washington, DC: Government Printing Office.

NATIONAL COMMISSION ON EXCELLENCE IN EDUCATION, (1983b), *Meeting the Challenge: Recent Reports to Improve Education Across the Nation*. Washington, DC: U.S. Department of Education, 15 November.

NATIONAL COMMISSION ON SECONDARY EDUCATION FOR HISPANICS, (1984), *Make Something Happen: Hispanics and Urban High School Reform*, (Volumes I and II), Washington, DC: Hispanic Policy Development Project.

NATIONAL SCIENCE BOARD COMMISSION, (1983), *Educating Americans for the 21st Century: A Plan of Action for Improving Mathematics, Science and Technology*

Education for all American Elementary and Secondary Students so that Their Achievement is the Best in the World by 1995. Washington, DC: National Science Board Commission on Precollegiate Education in Mathematics, Science and Technology, National Science Foundation.

NAYLOR, D.T. (1985), 'Reforming America's schools', *LRE Project Exchange*, 5(1), Winter.

THE NEW IMMIGRATION: A CHALLENGE TO AMERICAN SOCIETY, (1984), *Harvard Graduate Society Newsletter*, Spring/Summer, p. 9.

NICKERSON, R.S. (1982), *Understanding Understanding*, Cambridge, MA: Bolt, Beranek and Newman, July.

NICKERSON, R.S., PERKINS, D.N. and SMITH, E.E. (1984), *Teaching Thinking*. (Report No. 5575) Cambridge, MA: Bolt, Beranek and Newman, Inc, January.

ODDEN, A. (1984), 'Financing educational excellence', *Phi Delta Kappan*, 65(5), January, pp. 311–8.

OFFERMANN, D.A. (1984), 'Designing a general education curriculum for today's high school student', *Educational Leadership*, 41(6), March, pp. 50–4.

OLSON, D.R. (1973), 'What is worth knowing and what can be taught?' *School Review*, 82(11), pp. 27–43.

OLSON, D.R. (1976), 'Culture, technology and intellect', in RESNICK, L.B. (Ed.), *The Nature of Intelligence*. Hillsdale, NJ: Lawrence Erlbaum Associates, pp. 189–202.

PALINCSAR, A.S. and BROWN, A.L. (1984), 'Reciprocal teaching of comprehensive — fostering and comprehension monitoring activities', *Cognition and Instruction*, I(2), Spring, pp. 117–75.

PASSOW, A.H. (1976), *Secondary Education Reform: Retrospect and Prospect*. New York: Teachers College, Columbia University.

PASSOW, A.H. (1984a), *Reforming Schools in the 1980s: A Critical Review of the National Reports*, (report number 87), New York: ERIC Clearinghouse on Urban Education, April.

PASSOW, A.H. (1984b), *A Review of the Major Current Reports on Secondary Education*, (report number 88), New York: ERIC Clearinghouse on Unban Education, April.

PASSOW, A.H. (1984c), 'Tackling the reform reports of the 1980s', *Phi Delta Kappan*, 65(10), June, pp. 674–83.

PAULSON, D. and BALL, D. (1984), 'Back to basics: Minimum competency testing and its impact on minorities', *Urban Education*, 19(1), April, pp. 5–15.

PENFIELD, W. (1964), 'The uncommitted cortex', *Atlantic Monthly*, 214(1), July, pp. 77–81.

PENFIELD, W. (1975), *The Mystery of the Mind*, Princeton, NJ: Princeton University Press.

PETERSON, P.E. (1983a), *Background Paper* (published with *Making the Grade*). New York: The Twentieth Century Fund, pp. 23–174.

PETERSON, P.E. (1983b), 'Did the education commissions say anything?', *The Brookings Review*, 2(2), Winter, pp. 3–11.

POPULATION CHANGES WILL AFFECT EDUCATION POLICY, REPORT SAYS, (1984),

Report on Education Research, 16(7), 28 March, pp. 7–8.

PRESSEISEN, B.Z. (1982), *Understanding Adolescence: Issues and Implications for Effective Schools*. Philadelphia, PA: Research for Better Schools.

PURKEY, S.C. (1984), *School Improvement: An Analysis of an Urban School District Effective Schools Project*, Madison, WI: Wisconsin Center for Educational Research.

PREWITT-DIAZ, J.O. (1984), 'The immigration bill insults Hispanics', *Philadelphia Inquirer*, 29 June, p. 15A.

RADEST, H.B. (1983), 'Progressive education revisited', *Education Week*, II(35), 25 May, p. 24.

RANBOM, S. (1985), 'Schooling in Japan: The paradox in the pattern', *Education Week*, IV(22), 20 February, pp. 11–34.

RAVITCH, D. (1983a), *The Troubled Crusade: American Education 1945–1980*, New York, Basic Books.

RAVITCH, D. (1983b), 'On thinking about the future', *Phi Delta Kappan*, 64(5), January, pp. 317–20.

RAVITCH, D. (1983c), 'Forgetting the questions: The problem of educational reform', *Independent School*, 42(3), February, pp. 57–67.

RAVITCH, D. (1984a), 'Bring literature and history back to elementary schools', *Education Week*, III(16), 11 January, pp. 24.

RAVITCH, D. (1984b), 'The continuing crisis: Fashions in education', *The American Scholar*, 53(2), Spring, pp. 183–93.

RAYWID, M.A., TESCONI, JR., C.A. and WARREN, D.R. (1984), *Pride and Promise: Schools of Excellence for All the People*. Westbury, NY: American Educational Studies Association.

REAGAN, B.R. (1984), *Information Packet*, Philadelphia, PA: Conference for Urban Superintendents and Policy Makers, Research for Better Schools, (photocopy), 24–25 May.

REED, S. (1984), 'An effective teacher: The key ingredients', *The New York Times*, 15 April, pp. 36–37 and 72.

REPORT CARD: TEST SCORES FALL AND DROPOUT RATE RISES NATIONALLY, (1984), *Philadelphia Inquirer*, 6 January, pp. 1A and 4A.

RESNICK, D.P. and RESNICK, L.B. (1983), 'Improving educational standards in American schools', *Phi Delta Kappan*, 65(3), November, pp. 178–80.

ROBERTS, A.D. (1984), 'The ASCD high school network: Impressions from the road', *Educational Leadership*, 41(6), March, pp. 44–7.

RUBIN, L. (1983), *The Call for School Reform*, Portland, OR: Northwest Regional Exchange, December.

RUSSELL, R.L. and GINSBURG, H.P. (1984), 'Cognitive analysis of children's mathematics difficulties', *Cognition and Instruction*, 1(2), pp. 217–44.

RUTTER, M., MAUGHAM, B., MORTIMER, P. and OUSTON, J. with SMITH, A. (1979), *Fifteen Thousand Hours: Secondary Schools and Their Effects on Children*, Cambridge, MA: Harvard University Press.

SARASON, S.B. (1983), *Schooling in America: Scapegoat and Salvation*. New York: The Free Press.

SEELEY, D.S. (1984), 'Educational partnership and the dilemmas of school reform', *Phi Delta Kappan*, 65(6), February, pp. 383–8.

SENECHAL, M. and FLECK, G. (1985), Two-dimensional math in a three-dimensional world', *Education Week*, IV(20), 6 February, p. 40.

SERVICE AREAS TO EXCEED HIGH-TECH IN JOB GROWTH, (1984), *Education Week*, III(34), 16 May, p. 11.

SEVENER, D. (1984), 'Illinois board preparing reform plan for rugged test in state legislature', *Education Week*, III(37–38), 6 June, pp. 8 and 34.

SHABAD, T. (1984), 'Emigrés see merits and flaws in Soviet research', *New York Times*, 8 July, p.4.

SHANKER, A. (1984), 'Taking the measure of American education reform: An assessment of the education reports', *American Journal of Education*, 92(3), May, pp. 314–24.

SHIMAHARA, N.K. (1985), 'Japanese education and its implications for U.S. education', *Phi Delta Kappan*, 66(6), February, pp. 418–21.

SHIPP, E.R. (1984), 'Chicago's school chief is denied a new contract', *The New York Times*, 25 July, p. A12.

SHREEVE, W., *et. al.* (1984), 'Citizens and educators should assess local strengths in view of national reports', *NASSP Bulletin*, 68(470), March, pp. 30–6.

SIXTY-TWO PERCENT OF U.S. FAMILIES HAVE TWO INCOMES, REPORT SAYS, (1984), *Philadelphia Inquirer*, 2 April, p. 6A.

SIZER, T. (1977), 'Why the public school?', *The Principal*, 56(6), July–August, pp. 6–11.

SIZER, T.R. (1983a), *A Review and Comment on the National Reports*, Reston, VA: National Association of Secondary School Principals, 15 pp.

SIZER, T.R. (1983b), 'High school reform: The need for engineering', *Phi Delta Kappan*, 64(10), June, pp. 679–83.

SIZER, T.R. (1983c), 'Essential schools: A first look', *NASSP Bulletin*, 67(465), October, pp. 33–8.

SIZER, T.R. (1984a), *Horace's Compromise: The Dilemma of the American High School*, Boston: Houghton Mifflin.

SIZER, T.R. (1984b), 'A time for renewal', *Independent School*, 43(3), February, pp. 13–20 and 54–8.

SIZER, T.R. (1984c), 'Compromises', *Educational Leadership*, 41(6), March, pp. 34–7.

SIZER, T.R. (1984d), 'The secret ingredient: People', *The New York Times*, 15 April, p. 35.

SLAVIN, R.E. (1983), *Cooperatiave Learning*, New York: Longman.

SLOAN, D. (1984), 'On raising critical questions about the computer in education', *Teachers College Record*, 85(4), Summer, pp. 539–47.

SLOBODZIAN, J.A. (1984), 'N.J. 9th graders rate low in math in test's trial run', *Philadelphia Inquirer*, 12 July, p. 16BP.

SNOW, R.E. (1982), *Intelligence, Motivation, and Academic Work*, San Diego, CA paper presented to the National Commission for Excellence in Education, 30 July, 13 pp. (photocopy).

'SOCRATIC DIALOGUE' WITH DEREK BOK, (1984), *Harvard Graduate School of Education Association Bulletin*, XXVIII(3), Spring/Summer, p. 5.

SOLTIS, J.F. and TIMPANE, M. (1984), 'Cultivating a community of teaching', *Education Week*, III(32), 2 May, pp. 19 and 24.

SOUTHERN POLICYMAKERS WEIGH COLLEGE STUDENT ACHIEVEMENT TESTS,

(1984), *Report on Educational Research*, 16(14), July, pp. 5–7.

SPADY, W.G. and MARX, G. (1984), *Excellence in our Schools: Making it Happen*, Arlington, VA and San Francisco, CA: American Association of School Administrators and Far West Laboratory.

SPENCER, H. (1963), *Education: Intellectual, Moral, and Physical*, Paterson, NJ: Littlefield, Adams.

SPRING, J. (1984), 'Education and the Sony war', *Phi Delta Kappan*, 64(4), April, pp. 534–7.

STEDMAN, L.C. and SMITH, M.S. (1983), 'Recent reform proposals for American education', *Contemporary Education Review*, 2(2), Fall, pp. 85–104.

STEIN, B.J. (1983), '"A war with Japan? Really?" the "Astonishing ignorance" of some teen-agers', *Education Week*, III(8), 26 October, p. 18.

STERNBERG, R.J. (1981), 'Intelligence as thinking and learning skills', *Educational Leadership*, 39(1), October, pp. 18–20.

STEVENSON, B. (Ed.) (1976), *The Home Book of Quotations*, New York Dodd Mead, 10th Edition, originally published 1934.

STUDY WILL TRY TO IDENTIFY WHERE COLLEGES ARE WEAK, (1984), *Philadelphia Inquirer*, 6 August, p. 16F.

TANNER, D. (1982), 'The comprehensive high school in American education', *Educational Leadership*, 39(8), May, pp. 607–13.

TANNER, D. (1984), 'The American high school at the crossroads', *Educational Leadership*, 41(6), March, pp. 5–13.

TANNER, D. and TANNER, L.N. (1975), *Curriculum Development: Theory into Practice*, New York: Macmillan, Chapter 3: Curricular sources and influences — society, knowledge, and the learner, pp. 100–46.

TASK FORCE ON EDUCATION FOR ECONOMIC GROWTH, (1983), *Action for Excellence: A Comprehensive Plan to Improve our Nation's Schools*. Washington, DC: Education Commission of the States.

TEACHER EDUCATION TO BE STUDIED BY NATIONAL COMMISSION, (1984), *Report on Education Research*, 16(10), 9 May, p. 8.

THINKING SKILLS IN THE CURRICULUM, (1984), *Educational Leadership*, 42(1), September.

TOCH, T. (1984), 'For school reform's top salesmen. It's been some year', *Education Week*, III(37–38), 6 June, pp. 1 and 33.

TOCH, T. (1985), 'Governors warned school reform may be a two — edged sword', *Education Week*, IV(16), 9 January, pp. 1 and 11.

TRAVERS, K.J. and MCKNIGHT, C.C. (1985), 'Mathematics achievement in U.S. schools: Preliminary findings from the second IEA mathematics study', *Phi Delta Kappan*, 66(6), February, pp. 407–13.

THE TWENTIETH CENTURY FUND, (1983), *Making the Grade: Report of the Twentieth Century Fund Task Force on Federal Elementary and Secondary Education Policy*, New York: The Twentieth Century Fund.

TYACK, D. and HANSOT, E. (1982), 'Hard times, hard choices: The case for coherence in public school leadership', *Phi Delta Kappan*, 63(8), April, pp. 511–5.

TYE, B.B. (1984), 'Unfamiliar waters: Let's stop talking and jump in', *Educational Leadership*, 41(6), March, pp. 27–31.

TYLER, R.W. (1982), 'Dynamic response in a time of decline', *Phi Delta Kappan*, 63(10), June, pp. 655–8.

TYNER, H.A. (1984), 'Soviets turning a deaf ear to the computer boom', *Philadelphia Inquirer*, 22 June, p. 16A.

UNITED STATES DEPARTMENT OF EDUCATION, (1984), *The Nation Responds: Recent Efforts to Improve Education*. Washington, DC: U.S. Department of Education, May.

URBAN SCHOOLS: SOME STATISTICS, (1984), *Pera-Scope* (Pennsylvania Educational Research Association), Spring, p. 2.

U.S. GROWS OLDER, and MORE DIVERSE, (1984), *Philadelphia Inquirer*, 21 June, p. 4A.

USDAN, M.D. (1984), 'New trends in urban demography', *Educational and Urban Society*, 16(4), August, pp. 399–414.

VAUGHAN, J.C. (1984), 'Knowledge resources for improving the content of preservice teacher education', *Journal of Teacher Education*, XXXV(4), July/August, pp. 3–8.

VON BERGEN, D. (1984), 'Automation will cost jobs, U.S. study says', *Philadelphia Inquirer*, 11 May, p. 13C.

WAGNER, R.K. and STERNBERG, R.J. (1984), 'Alternative conceptions of intelligence and their implications for education', *Review of Educational Research*, 54(2), Summer, pp. 179–223.

WALTON, S. (1984), 'Experts seek to shift focus of reforms to content, texts', *Education Week*, 28 March, p. 1 and 15.

WHEN TEACHERS TACKLE THINKING SKILLS, (1984), *Educational Leadership*, 42(3), November.

WHIMBEY, A. and WHIMBEY, L.S. (1975), *Intelligence Can Be Taught*, New York: E.P. Dutton.

WHITE, E. (1984), 'Education's troubled crusade: No easy victories, no lasting defeats', *Education Week*, III(16), 11 January, pp. 8 and 17.

WHITEHEAD, A.N. (1929), *The Aims of Education*, New York: Macmillan.

WHY TEACHERS FAIL: HOW TO MAKE THEM BETTER, (1984), *Newsweek*, 24 September, pp. 64–70.

WHY U.S. INDUSTRY IS COMING HOME, (1984), *Harper's Magazine*, 268(1607), April, p. 14.

WILLIAMS, E. (1984), 'Joe Jones: A dropout turns into a scholar', *Philadelphia Inquirer*, 14 August, p. 3B.

WITT, E. (1984), 'Gains in the classroom reported', *Philadelphia Inquirer*, 31 July, p. 3A.

YANKELOVICH, SKELLY and WHITE, INC, (1984), *Spanish USA 1984*, New York: Yankelovich, Skelly and White.

THE YELLOW PAGES IN L.A. SOON TO HAVE SPANISH EDITION, (1984), *Philadelphia Inquirer*, 5 July, p. 22C.

YOUNG, J.H. (1979), 'Teacher participation in curriculum decision making: An organizational dilemma', *Curriculum Inquiry*, 9(2), Summer, p. 113.

YUDOF, M.G. (1984), 'Educational policy research and the new consensus of the 1980s', *Phi Delta Kappan*, 65(7), March, pp. 456–9.

INDEX